A CHILDHOOD IN THE MILKY WAY

Ohio History and Culture

Series on Ohio History and Culture

David Brendan Hopes

A CHILDHOOD IN
THE MILKY WAY

Becoming a Poet in Ohio

The University of Akron Press Akron, Ohio

Portions of this books appeared as essays in the following publications or anthologies: *The Sacred Place* (University of Utah Press), *Writer's Digest, Writer's Yearbook 1994, The Conservationist, Southern Environmental, Timbuktu, Ohio Magazine, New Letters, Sycamore Review.*

All inquiries and permissions requests should be addressed to the publisher, The University of Akron Press, Akron, OH 44325–1703.

Manufactured in the United States of America

FIRST EDITION 1999

03 02 01 00 99   5 4 3 2 1

LIBRARY OF CONGRESS CATALOGING IN PUBLICATION DATA
Hopes, David B.
    A Childhood in the Milky Way : becoming a poet in
  Ohio / David Brendan Hopes
        p. cm.—(Ohio history and culture)
    ISBN 1-884836-45-3 (cloth : alk. paper).—ISBN 1-884836-46-1
  (pbk. : alk. paper)
    1. Hopes, David B.—Childhood and youth. 2. Hopes, David
  B.—Homes and haunts—Ohio—Akron. 3. Poets, American—
  20th century—Biography. 4. Akron (Ohio)—Social life and
  customs. I. Title. II. Series.
  PS3558.06343Z464 1999
  811'.54—DC21
  [B]   99-10712
                                                  CIP

The paper used in this publication meets the minimum requirements of American National Standard for Information Science—Permanence of Paper for Printed Library Materials, ANSI Z39.48—1984.∞

This book is for Linda

We all know the fable of Aesop about the dog who was fortunate to find a delicious bone. As he was crossing a stream on his way home, he looked in the water and saw another dog very like himself with another bone, which he coveted. He opened his mouth to add the other dog's bone to his hoard, and his own dropped into the water, swirling downstream to be lost. The dog's mistake was more basic than greed for two bones rather than one. His mistake was forgetting that his central need was not to possess, but to devour.

CONTENTS

PREFACE

By the time one reaches adolescence, one is a committee. So many textures of personality have been scratched into the surface, so many accommodations have been made to suit circumstance, employment, companions, that it is difficult to remember who you were when you started out, or who you intended to be at the end. That I began as a goofy kid in the brawling neighborhoods of Akron, Ohio, and ended up who I am, has always been, until now, a paradox not much thought of, even by myself, but much present in dreams and in the strange, interdimensional moments before the writing of a poem.

Commencing *A Childhood in the Milky Way* allowed me to open pages of my life that the very circumstances of my life had obscured: that I was by phases an intellectual and crudely anti-intellectual; that I was something of a homegrown mystic, and yet, perhaps not surprisingly, wildly contemptuous of homegrown mysticism; at times a predatory voluptuary; that I was, at the base of bases, a poet, an artist without ever thinking much about what it *meant* to be an artist—all of this had something to do with how and where I grew up, with the city in Ohio I abandoned with alacrity and, of course, to which have I have returned again and again with growing fascination and regard.

When my sister and I were very young, we would load up the car with ourselves and our parents and our grandparents—

Mother's mother and father—and our luggage, and our effervescent expectations, and set out on the new Eisenhower highways for points unknown, certain that however pathetic the Indian fort or Cheese Festival or Mennonite village or presidential monument to which we were headed was, it would be better, more chocked with basic information, than the streets we had left. It never crossed my mind, not once, that if I were living in Twinsburg or East Liverpool, even Chicago or New York, I might long to go to Akron, once, to know what strange things unfolded there.

I was one strange thing unfolding there. Whoever thought that process might turn out to be *interesting?*

This is a book of memory. Where it deviates from history, you must excuse it. History deviates from history; a poet is simply more honest about it.

This is a book about a rough kid who becomes a poet, a playwright, a painter, having known none of those things in youth, yet somehow sensing how and why to do them through the mute earth under his feet. The book is, for me, a sacrament of remembrance, as I claim in the text that poetry itself is. I have changed the names in the book, to satisfy questions of legal liability, but I think those who might recognize themselves would be joyful, as I am in the recollection of them.

I still seldom bring myself to say in daily life, "I am a poet." The Midwestern habit of circumspection is too ingrained. But, in the watches of the night, even an Ohio boy can think of what has come to pass and be amazed, not at what he has accomplished so much as what he has stumbled into. The opportunity to embody one's labor is a blessing, though as an absolute it precludes other equally desirable absolutes. I cannot be a great lover. The problem is not *mechanical,* mind you, but that my full attention would never be on the beloved's self, but on what could be made of it all later. I cannot be a saint, and I would like to be. Yahweh and Apollo make absolute demands. You can serve two great masters only if you intend to cheat them both. I am a poet. For the sake of my own sanity, I have stopped enumerating the things that leaves out. We poets flatter ourselves that we can slight the everyday because we shall go glittering through the treetops, useless and gorgeous, singing. The truth is probably much plainer, and much luckier. It is work. Plain work. And the strength for it comes from the ground on which you were born, however surprising that seems in retrospect.

One can begin to sound like a sage by just sitting and recording pairs of mutually exclusive ideals. We cannot both taste and anticipate. We cannot both judge and perceive at one moment, not at once grow and foster growth. We must choose whether to be just or lawful, fanatical or devout. We cannot stand at once for peace and for power. The sword behind our backs negates the outstretched hand. We cannot stand at once for culture and money. We cannot at once champion profit and equality. Justice cannot filibuster; mercy cannot equivocate. If you are filibustering in the cause of justice, equivocating in the cause of mercy, warring on behalf of peace, you need to look at yourself hard, for you are separating means and ends, a division which usually—if not quite inevitably—leads to the creation of monsters. The vocation of the artist is to choose a path to follow, and to follow it with the glittering-eyed dedication of a saint—whether otherwise he be saint or no—realizing that the huddle to whom he will be magnificent will be crowded off most thoroughfares by the throng who thinks he is a fool.

The vocation of the artist involves the putting away of such regrets as are not useful in eternity. Somewhere within must lie the power to call our loneliness chastity, our poverty austerity, our terror faith. This is not merely disguise; it is transformation.

❄

I would like to acknowledge as necessary to the completion of this book the offices of an outstanding editor, Elton Glaser, and the encouragement of John Fleischman of *Ohio Magazine*.

Also, in ways I need not specify, but which they will understand, Nancy Jo Niehoff, Viola Deppen, Helen Otto, Sandra Davidson, Hale Chatfield, David Fratus, Philip Booth, Arthur Hoffman, Thomas Dolce, Steven Maltbie, Carol Donley, Sandra Glass, Ellen Pfirrmann. Also thanks to my colleagues at the University of North Carolina Literature and Language Department, who have tolerated me and encouraged me with time through many projects, not the least the making of this book.

A CHILDHOOD IN THE MILKY WAY

1. FOUNDERS

For an age, and then an age, the waters touched the waters.
There was no voice, neither bird nor spirit.
Then the waters parted from the waters.
We were there in our dry skins and our bewildered eyes.
We did what they did not expect of us.
We sang.

IF YOU WENT the farthest you could go down Goodview Avenue without your father there to hold your hand, you would look down from the hill that was your whole world into a shallow, wide depression: the valley of the Little Cuyahoga. From the valley by day came the rumble of trains in the switching yards, and flashes from the sides of automobiles running Mogadore Road to Market Street and on downtown. Far to the west, the smokestacks of Goodyear Tire lofted a cloud that only later would cry ecological calamity, but which was then the roof under which your father and the fathers of everyone you knew earned your bread. The Tower Building, Saint Bernard's, the massed cylinders of the Quaker Oats elevators were sometimes visible if the leaves were fallen and the perspective was right, though they might as well be the far side of the moon for all their strangeness and the daily unlikelihood that you would ever get close to them.

In the gathering twilight, before the street lamps were lit and it was still all right for a boy to be abroad, lights began to glitter beyond the Little Cuyahoga: busses, taxis, trains, tiny surreptitious sparks in the near forest, the swinging blue and red lanterns that boyish folklore averred belonged to the railroad bulls who would knock you out, tie you up, and cart you off to servitude somewhere out West if they caught you near the tracks. This was not an altogether horrendous prospect.

As night deepened, what you saw became less important and what you heard, more. You had to go home when the streetlamps flickered on, but if you had any imagination, you could picture what went on in the ravines and the patches of dark woods that led down to the Little Cuyahoga, and could almost see where the spangled streets led as well—to the great, gathering brightness on the bottoms of low clouds, which you knew was Downtown, even if you seldom went there.

If there were guests in the house, you could tell whether they were from the neighborhood. When the trains smashed together in the coupling yards, visitors would jump and spill their coffee, while we natives smiled and gave each other that look of acknowledgment. Trains were thundering in the night mist from the Little Cuyahoga, and it would not be altogether truthful to say we no longer noticed them, but rather that they had become part of the fabric of our unconscious. Like city people suddenly countrified, we missed the metallic din when we couldn't hear it, though we did not necessarily know what it was we missed, nor where to go to get back to it.

Nobody I knew went back more than a generation in Akron. Some of us were not that much longer in America. Mother's mother had come from County Clare via Toronto, Ohio. Mother's father from County Tyrone via Tyrone, Pennsylvania. Father's parents went back across the same water, but when and where they did not tell me. The verb most apt for our advent was "to flee." The fathers of our neighborhood fled from the coal-fields of Pennsylvania and the exhausted farms of West Virginia, as their fathers had from famine in Ireland and tumult in Poland and the Ukraine. Everything we looked on was new, suspicious, alternately desirable and contemptible. Perhaps those would be good words to describe us, too. We didn't know if we wanted to stay where we were, or if we would be allowed to. Some of us decided to hold our breaths until we could flee again. Some of us decided to abide, for a while anyway, and be as happy as it was our lot to be.

In ancient photos, my mother's father and his brothers glare out from their hilly fields with the glowering dark beauty of movie stars. The women these men marry are fragile as porcelain.

The house of the son of Akron's founder, Simon Perkins, still stands. Each year until junior high—after which time they figured immovable cynicism had set in—our teachers made us pilgrims to that shrine where our city was born. We witnessed life and luxury in the far-off days of the Connecticut Western Reserve, where Greek revival farmhouses and the Imperial ideal flourished side by side, where midway through the eighteenth century the insatiate colonies of the seaboard reached as far as the British crown, Virginia and Carolina colliding, on paper, with the great Bourbon expanse of Louisiana.

Connecticut claimed the wilderness south of Lake Erie, a land cut by narrow rivers and haunted by the ghosts of Indians. When you were very young, you allowed your father to drag you to the YMCA to join the Indian Guides, a mildly humiliating enterprise which you tolerated because it provided names like Mingo and Chippewa and Erie and Algonquin to haunt the imagination. You looked on maps of their empires and wanderings to see which of them might have inhabited the land you knew. You found arrowheads at the curves of streams and at the bottoms of ploughed furrows. You picked barrels of muskets, rusted thin as paper, from the middens of vanished farms. It was a black, glaciered, watered land reclaimed each spring by forests of oak, maple, and chestnut which, reborn with the seasons, covered and forgave all. You scanned the sky for the golden eagles from whose feathers ceremonial headdresses were made, and almost thought you saw them, almost twisted the words in the Peterson bird guide successfully around to verify your claim. It was so rich that, during the infamous Hinckley hunt, settlers piled slaughtered wolves and bear and deer fifteen feet high against their sheds for a generation, until the wild land was "tamed."

It was not always the Mid–, but once the Far West. We learned in Ohio history class in junior high that, between 1789 and 1807, the effective western boundary of the United States was Portage Path, which was still a frontier in my time, if not between white and Indian, then between middle and upper middle class. The times we went to West Hill when I was a child, crossing that ancient frontier, could be counted on one hand.

In a meadow on the flat plain of the Cuyahoga in Cascade Valley Park stands an ancient trident oak, trained by the Indians to mark the point at which one carried one's canoe overland from the Cuyahoga to the Tuscarawas, using the depressions of the Portage Lakes southward to ease the way. To go from the Cuyahoga to the Tuscarawas is to shift from the watershed of the Great Lakes and the St. Lawrence to the watershed of the Mississippi—a crossroads in pre-Columbian times of unparalleled significance, the Suez of the Delawares and the Iroquois.

As a boy, my longing for a time machine was almost unendurable. My friends, naming the ways in which I am still a twelve-year-old, generally leave this fact out, but it is the first thing I would mention. I knew Chapel Hill when it was a huge shopping mall, where we junior high kids finally had a place to hang, the downtown streets being off-limits long ago. When I learned it was called that because there had been a chapel there, a place of worship for the Indians, I didn't stop cruising, but I did so with my eyes strained to the point of Superman x-ray devices, trying to peer through the polished floor at footprints, arrowheads, bloodstains, at the remnants of the unaccountable things those distant people might have called worship.

❄

I forget why Simon Perkins built a city on our spur of land rising sufficiently above the surrounding plains to justify the Greek name *akros,* the high place—but it must have had something to do with money. The town of Middlebury—absorbed and nameless but for a tiny park beside a fire station that was once the Middlebury town square—materialized first. As a kid, I scooted under the fence of Middlebury cemetery to look at tombstones whose eroding inscriptions bore birth dates in the eighteenth century. For a boy hungering after antiquities weighed in the scale of Nineveh and Troy, this was a disappointment, but the best that could be had. Resenting the newness of our history, I made up my own, imagining a tumbled wall or a weed-grown arch as a remnant of undiscovered civilizations. A ridge between lawns marked an imperial parade. White stones taken from a tumbled temple were worked, unbeknownst to later men, into a savings and loan facade. Had I been less ignorant, I would have known of the Mound Builders, the mysterious first-comers of that part of the world, whose antiquity and engineering skills were nearly of European stature. I wanted kings, and heroes in bronze; what I got was hunters wrapped in skins moving stealthily through an endless forest. One should have been just as good as the other, but somehow it didn't work that way, and every trip to the library deepened my grievance against my home sod. I was born to bathe in the soft gleam of antiquity. Everything around me was new, raw, unpoetic.

Middlebury and Brittain and Cascade and other hamlets

swallowed by the growing adolescent Akron gave their names to streets or neighborhoods or parking lots or were forgotten. We followed a canal to this high place in the middle of the woods, a canal which linked us with the highways of commerce to the northeast and the southwest. A canalboat took six hours to pass through Akron, which was by the standard of the day, I suppose, greased lightning.

The Civil War, elsewhere such a disaster, enriched the pockets of the city fathers and the reputation of Akron as a hotbed of civil rights; Simon Perkins's neighbors were stations of the Underground Railroad; Sojourner Truth raised her voice from the High Street Universalist Church in a ringing endorsement of the rights of women. Industry followed, and Seiberling and Firestone, then bitter labor disputes poetically cited by Steinbeck in *The Grapes of Wrath* as the beginning of American blue-collar consciousness.

Akron's eminence was as rawboned as its origins, and her citizens took pride in the oddest of her distinctions. Mr. Harper, who lived with his daughter at the other end of Goodview Avenue, said—face shining with pride—that during his hobo days in the Depression, Akron's reputation was so rough that only the young and pugnacious would get off the train here. If you could fight, maybe you could thrive. You could still see then the dimming marks where vagrants signaled their brothers as to which houses were hospitable, which not, which had vicious dogs, police, or contained a soft heart.

My mother bragged that Akron was, after New York and Detroit, third on Hitler's list of American cities to be bombed.

"Oh, I suppose the Stukas will fly over Pittsburgh and Philadelphia and D.C. in their hurry to get here," I scoffed, "and then over Cleveland to get to Detroit." Mother's civic pride remained undaunted by my superior knowledge of geography.

In her time, the city divided into neighborhoods along lines of ethnic origin. This tended to divide people according to religion as well, and there were recognizable Catholic neighborhoods around Saint Vincent's and Annunciation and Saint Mary's. One could burn a cross on North Hill and be sure that Italian eyes would see it. Shouting "Hunky" or "Hillbilly" from a corner in our neck of the woods, Goodyear Heights, would get a reaction unless you were clearly one of "us." Out towards west Akron, blood grew bluer, and the white spires of solvent Protestantism punched through the roof of elms.

State of origin was almost as powerfully symbolic a division as nation. Though now I'm not exactly clear how we used the information, we knew precisely whose parents had come from Pennsylvania, whose from West Virginia, whose from the South. Other places of origin might as well have been extraterrestrial. Karl, in my third grade class, was from *Massachusetts,* an unheard-of place, a shadowy Thule where everyone ran around in great gray Puritan hats starving in the cold and giving sermons, and, what with the outlandishness of his origins and his grating, Bobby Kennedy accent, it was good he only stayed a year, for he would never have fit in. Sherry from Alabama had it a little better, for not only were we enamored of her beauty and her molasses vowels, but Alabama was the sort of place we sensed that we—even we—might fitly look down upon.

Our neighborhood possessed its special kind of chaos. By that I imply not disorder, but an order deriving little from what would, a few blocks away, be thought of as reality. We were the blue-eyed strivers. Not quite white trash. Certainly not the aristocracy of west Akron. We were an embattled lower middle class fighting like hell to get to the middle ground. In this, we were most like the blacks in the neighborhoods to the west and south, who were our natural allies even as they were our social adversaries. It was they whom we most mistrusted, wanting the same things as they did, fearing there wouldn't be enough for everybody.

Getting ahead was the goal, though no two people agreed

on what getting ahead looked like, and for every one who said the key was education, another said it was money or who you knew or the sort of luck that rains on the adaptable. Some threw up their hands and said it was birth, and about that nothing could be done but lie. We were Machiavellian out of ignorance rather than intention. If someone else wants it, it must be good. Never be content. Join. Test. Discard. Try everything, and, if something works, go with it hell-for-leather.

Second-generation immigrants were Democrats. We, whose families had scrabbled about in the Appalachian hills perhaps a generation longer, and who had therefore larger equity in the American Dream, were Republicans. My mother's family, farmers and then rubber workers, hated FDR with an unaccountable hatred. My first conception of FDR was not as an American president at all, but as a sort of clown, a pinkish national embarrassment, with a sidekick named Falla. It was fascinating discovering the more general understanding of this man and his values as time went on. I thought for a while their attitude amounted to mere cussed opposition to anything that was good for you— which I understand because I inherited some—but I think rather it was that here were some among us who seemed actually to think that identifying with gentry made us gentry.

My extended family's view of things, and the views of the families around us, were not without imagination. They were in some senses, such as the FDR phantasm just related, quite fanciful. I seize on this observation as a way of explaining what happened to me. The will to become an artist firmed in me so early and with such lack of precedence in my environment that the only viable explanation is true inspiration, if not, as already observed, a congenital gesture of cussedness. Perhaps I was simply so dissatisfied with everything that I determined to become the one thing that nobody I knew was. The first time I ever remember being asked what I was going to be when I grew up, I answered, "an artist," by which I meant then a painter, an ambition founded upon my delight in the paintings in the lobby of our family doctor's office, and calculated, even if quite true, to raise the steepest edge of concern in my hearers.

Mother had a cousin who was a painter, whom I never met, referred to by her family at once with respect and with a look of wry mutual understanding and a slight flutter of wrists that gave one to understand that he was not quite "right," not quite one of "us." "Artistic" meant two things back then, and one had nothing to do with pens and brushes. Otherwise, the horizon loomed so emptily that the impression I developed about art and artists was not adversarial but simply blank. Art was what was done elsewhere by people unlike us. It was, therefore, desirable before all things.

Artists we thought we understood—Robert Frost, Norman Rockwell, Aaron Copland—were idolized without being really *used,* like Sunday suits hanging in the closet until they were too small and out of style. In father's locked file cabinet lay a leather-bound book with gold trim and golden end pages, at which one was allowed to look only occasionally and with adult supervision. It was called *Leaves of Gold* and contained poems. The fact that, upon later inspection, this proved a hilarious collection of the sappiest inspirational doggerel was irrelevant to a child who, at the first, came to associate poetry with a holy removal, with something hidden and strange. For this object, desired above all things, the lock would be tested, the door surreptitiously opened, and the precious volume cradled in the arms without one's even daring to open the cover.

Mother had some Gainsborough reproductions of upper-class little British girls, and father hung a Rockwell Kent tree by the front door. I don't know why. Did they *like* them? They never mentioned them except to find places for them when we moved. That someone might turn to art as a life's work was an idea not so much scorned as simply not considered. When I discovered Mother had met Hart Crane, even knew who he was when I mentioned the name, I was numb from envy, and then from despair that she could tell me nothing more than one would say of an eccentric neighbor. She did not fully believe me when I told her of the swath he cut through American letters. He was the candy man, the strange, handsome purveyor of sundries at a downtown drugstore.

Other people who grew up when and where I did will protest. They will name all the artistic opportunities available. Yeah, well they lived in another neighborhood. *We* didn't look on these opportunities as "art" so much as exploration of foreign territory. My friend Mike was German and Croatian, and, if you went to a wedding with him, or to a family party, you could get a dose of folk dancing and strange, spicy foods, the names of which you could not pronounce. The old ones would speak in the tongues of their fatherlands. If you went into the homes of Catholic friends—which would, at first, be a frightening experience—you could see holy images: Jesus pointing to his naked heart, or Mary in a blue dress, holding a lily and looking up at the sky. I longed for one of these florid images, and, when I asked for one, my parents reacted with a revulsion that but made them the more attractive.

You could take drawing lessons at the Akron Art Institute on Saturday morning. It was a different age, and your parents would give you money to take the bus by yourself all the way downtown. You might begin by faithfully attending the drawing class, but it wouldn't take long to understand that it wasn't really for you. There were the serious students up front, near the teacher, who had come month after month and knew what he meant when he said "nib" or "crosshatch." Behind them were the rowdies, who had to be stopped again and again from racing around in the galleries, terrifying the other patrons with their noise and velocity. Eventually you just drifted away. You drifted down two blocks to Howard Street. You drifted there because it was a perilous magnet, because it was forbidden, because you sensed in your heart that there the life of a spirit wholly unlike yours lay hidden. Before urban renewal gutted it, Howard Street was the hub of African-American culture in Akron, and also the place where you reputedly would find what parents vaguely deemed "trouble." There was a bus stop in front of the Diamond Market, the very center of Howard Street, and that was your excuse. You would stand there in the snow, taking it all in. Sometimes you would enter the forbidding Diamond Market—which was, after all, just a grocery store—and everything seemed new and strange because black people were handling it, putting things on the shelves and taking them off again, and you had never seen that before. If you wanted to buy a Three Musketeers, you would hand the money to a black man, and he would hand back the change. This was amazing to me. The snow would fall, and you would wait for the red and yellow lights of the bus to loom through the pale swirl, and you would be thinking how few things were the way people told you they would be.

A racial slur, or even a slighting comment, would never have been tolerated around my mother or father. My mother was often sick, and housekeepers, usually black, were hired to help her with the work of raising a family. With them, and with all people of color who entered our sphere, there was the strictest code of respect. That they should not eat at table with us or be called "Mrs." was not even considered. And yet, one could hardly say we were without the taint of racism. I don't know where it came from; it probably didn't have to come from anywhere but merely seeped in from the atmosphere through which the Midwestern, white middle class struggled its way forward. I went to Akron public schools for twelve years and graduated from Ellet High

School without once having a black child in my class. I grew up afraid of black men and boys, and only as an adult—when I actually met some—did that fear atrophy.

And yet I had also for a while the innocence by which racism and all other prejudice must one day finally be conquered, an innocence to which the difference between white and black is purely one of color. I lost this innocence without really understanding what was happening.

I went to church camp for several summers at Camp Templed Hills in Brinkhaven, Ohio. You will hear more of this place later. I usually came home with addresses of fellow campers with whom I would be pen pals for a season or so, until other friends and activities intervened. One summer, there was a girl from Columbus whom I especially liked. We wrote off and on, and I invited her to visit Akron, and she invited me to visit Columbus. My trip to Columbus to see Debra almost happened, as the family was headed there anyway for the State Fair. But I showed mother a snapshot I had taken of Debra at camp. Debra was black. There was silence on the subject of Columbus for a while. Then the minister from church made a visitation to talk to me about what was socially acceptable, and how sometimes a loving impulse had to be checked by the wise standards of the community. I had no idea what he was talking about. He had to say the phrase, "your little friend, Debra," before it dawned on me what I could have done to offend community standards.

For several years, I was a member of Goodyear Boy Scout Troop 40. I became an eagle scout and was senior patrol leader for so long that people forgot anyone else had done the job. I won the Litchfeld Award that Goodyear gave to the outstanding scout of the year, and my name was in bronze in the lobby of Goodyear Hall, under the murals of angels leading martyred soldiers from the wrack of Word War I, until the room was redecorated and wood panels covered my glory. But when I was a tenderfoot, with a new uniform and a throng of delicious new activities, I made an interesting mistake. Goodyear had a basketball team then, and it was the pride of the Goodyear scouts to carry flags at the opening ceremonies for the team's games. One afternoon, I, having carried the American flag and being, therefore, the celebrity of the next few hours, was approached by a boy who said we looked wonderful out there on the polished floor, and he wanted to be one of us. I invited him to the troop meeting the next Monday night. He showed up, and all hell broke loose. He was black. I can say honestly that it never crossed my mind, and yet whatever power of excuse those words carried is mitigated by the fact that it has crossed my mind forever after.

Neither the minister nor the scoutmasters were bad men. None of them would have tolerated blatant hatred or racism. My basketball buddy did get into the scouts, for Goodyear sponsored an all-black troop, a gesture of extreme liberality at the time. And yet, for me, the pattern was set. They were different, and, if I didn't remember the difference at all times, I would be humiliated by "my own." Even my adventures on Howard Street couldn't reverse this, for they were *adventures,* journeys into otherness where I would never be quite at home, where neither side, in fact, wanted me to be quite at home.

For many years, I kept the postcard Debra sent me when, my face burning red with shame, I wrote to tell her I would not be meeting her in Columbus. It said simply, "I understand."

2 . FIRE AND ICE

We are fire in green gloves, wind in a cup of flowers,
bulging what the snow beat flat.
Green, the glacier's daughters, giving back. . . .
We have made ourselves from nothing.

THE HILLS WE LIVED ON were our true heritage. Why didn't anyone explain this to us? They were not just hills. They had moved here, like us. The very stones under our heels were immigrants. Snaking across northern Ohio, the terminal moraine is the skeleton of an ice monster a mile high. Why isn't an image of this, of a blue frozen wall mounting ten times over the Cleveland Terminal Tower, given to every Ohio child at birth, so that we may know what we escaped by a few mere millennia?

The Ice Age is recent geological memory and, more frequently than people understand, an element of human memory. Deep melt waters from the glacier are still with us, pools gouged by thousand-foot waterfalls, craters left when the very rocks were moved, still freezing and thawing with the seasons. One such pool, Blue Pond, lay across from the apartment house my parents brought me to when I was born. Over part of Blue Pond some entrepreneur had built a dance hall on pilings driven into the glacial mud. A trolley line ended at the dance hall, and, of a Saturday night, the area was busy with sheiks and shebas and the young in all their finery. One night, the trolley overshot and, instead of stopping at the end of the track, careered into the dance hall, throwing it from its pilings and sinking all the dancers into the depths of the pond. Or so Mother said. I tell this story having heard it many times and hoping it is true. What is verifiable is that at the edge of Blue Pond, among the cattails and blackbirds, are rotting stumps of pilings. It would be well for the glacier to have this triumph after all the years.

Goodview Avenue, the first home I remember, perches on the side of the moraine rumpled by the Wisconsin Ice Sheet. Only one side of the street was good for building. The other was essentially a cliff wall, and those who came a little later than we and had to perch on the cliff served as a sort of geological underclass. Left on its own, nature would plunge their houses to destruction a century or so before ours.

Adelaide Hill slopes down gently on the southeast corner. Pilgrim Hill on the northeast, however, is a sheer drop, a glacial convulsion, an asphalt rollercoaster lined with jumbly stairstep houses like pictures of villages in Switzerland. Steep, windy in all seasons, blacktopped, it formed the principal event of our walk home from Betty Jane School. You could make the ascent less grueling if you stayed to the ditches on either side, open storm sewers that gave the option of a broken landscape of rock and hollow instead of the implacable macadam climb of the pavement. The ditches provided not greater ease, but greater interest, to distract attention from your agony.

Parents warned incessantly against the ditches, for reasons still unclear. Certainly one was safer there than in the street, where in winter even skillful drivers squeezed their wheels and tapped their brakes in time to the terrible dance of the ices. Perhaps it had something to do with the "visibility syndrome" that pervades parenthood and to which the rest of the world is generally immune. The visibility syndrome dictates that a child must be physically visible—or, at the very least, audible—whenever a parent's anxiety level reaches a set but ineffable point. You remember the horror-stricken parental faces when, after hours of shopping, you went to play under the coat racks and were not available the instant it occurred to them to turn and look. You remember father's bellow over the waters of the lake, "Come here where I can see you."

You answer, "You can see us already."

"I need to see you better. And no diving unless you tell me first."

You remember your mother's voice over the rooftops, just loud enough that the matter could not be discerned, only that unmistakable note of adult hysteria. You run. You arrive panting on the doorstep, only to hear, "Just checking," she oblivious to the humiliation of being summoned from games by one's irrational mother.

Parents cherish this power, like so many Fausts able to conjure demons from the air with a word.

The Pilgrim Hill ditches made it necessary, however, for parental eyes to shift to the left or right to find us. They wanted us straight ahead, on dead level, at high noon. We were firmly admonished to keep to a preselected route between home and school, without short cuts or deviations, so that in case of an emergency we could be located quickly.

I don't know what they expected. That was the age of duck-and-cover, so perhaps they wanted to gather us in their arms in the last instant before the white blast of the Bomb. We suspected it had to do with an overall parental control psychosis, and, for the sake of self-assertion, we deviated where we could, whether it lengthened or shortened the way.

Pilgrim Hill, however, could not be wholly avoided. For a while, big boys from the neighborhood lingered in ambush at the bottom, like lions at a watering hole. The torment they inflicted seemed preordained, a rite of passage. Certainly their attitude implied they were perfectly within their rights. I did not yet recognize their identity with the trolls and black knights lurking at bridges and crossroads in stories, ready to exact indignities and thwart the way. I believe, however, that I forgave them even then for their archetypal stature. Their attacks dismayed us, but they never seemed unfair or unexpected. *Oh yes. We were wondering when this would happen.* They gave you the choice of outrunning them or of carrying them up Pilgrim Hill on your back. I couldn't outrun anybody, so I chose to bear, amazed and relieved at being able to do so.

It did not occur to us to protest these things. The world was the world. Also, their torment provided the occasion when I first realized I am stronger than I ought to be. Through time I send the bullies belated thanks; this is one of the Nine Great Lessons: your resources are greater than you think they are.

Until they are less. But that is a matter for adulthood.

Like all isolated hills, ours tended to develop its own biota, its own subspecies of the blue-collar *Homo sapiens* that were, with the elms and squirrels, the chief inhabitants of Goodyear Heights. My family formed its own tiny variation within the subspecies. We were Protestants in a heavily Central European Catholic quarter. My father was an office worker packed in among truck drivers and tire builders and a surprising percentage of honky-tonk musicians. Sometimes at night the twang of the steel guitar drifted from the Stewart's house next door; Mr. Porter down the street put on a tuxedo and a pink ruffled shirt to play "The Tennessee Waltz" at high school dances. People round about came home drunk from weddings and funerals alike, a sight which amazed me, for we had finger sandwiches and mints in little cups and sweet red cold punch at the one, and hearty Christian casseroles at the other.

We were heady and our neighbors emotional, a difference I

noticed but didn't have the vocabulary to describe. That's not to say we were better educated than our neighbors, but that we founded our virtues and prejudices on what we thought rather than what we felt. We were not *intellectual,* actually, but rather *antiemotional.* We mistook emotional inarticulateness for restraint. I've probed back though our generations to see who was at fault, but, of course, nobody was. Some think, some feel. This is an eternal aspect of Order. The fact that I was essentially an emotional child growing up in an unemotional household made things confusing for me, but, paradoxically, it has made adulthood easier. I've seldom regretted the ingrained reflex of passing my emotions before the light of reason before expressing them. What I have lost in spontaneity, I mostly regain in the strengthened—if slightly theatrical—power of the second thought, the doing after judgment exactly what you would have done before, emboldened, if anything, by consideration.

When I was six, my sister was born, and the Three Separate Kingdoms of my parents and me became Four, gathered if by bizarre treaty under one roof. Almost from the start, we took solitary, individual paths, and our frequent efforts at family unity sparked by some family activity had an aspect of artificiality, even of desperation. If all of us were gathered together at the same place at the same time, it was certain that one of us would be writhing inwardly with embarrassment. We sat behind our closed bedroom doors while our neighbors concentrated their energies on brawling, overcrowded families—violent, exclusive, supportive—the kind that made you feel suffocated when you went to visit, with their hugging and shouting and the spice of their food, and lonely when you returned to the quiet of your own house.

A friend once came to stay with us while his parents went through some turmoil. He told us later that his school grades had gone up that marking period because there was nothing to do at our house but study. My father took that as a compliment.

What I am saying is that I grew up in a situation as unpoetical as possible. Nobody got into trouble. However much they might think about it, nobody did anything that might embarrass, or that might give occasion for later embarrassment. One kept one's wild oats for sowing later, when they could do the most harm. One hid one's best and worst moments alike. Not turmoil, not tragedy, not upheaval, but this dull null is the worst of all possible cradles for art.

Art was not opposed—opposition is a form of energy—but simply ignored. Passions were an embarrassment; little ones were to be concealed or transmuted into material achievement; the great ones, the soul shatterers, were for people in the movies. The least poetical of all sensations—worse even than boredom—is a sense of displacement, and *that* we had to peddle. No books, no talk at home, no talk at school of the life of the mind. Not discouraged, simply not considered.

For this reason, I believe the urge to make poetry is innate. Nothing there or then would have suggested the idea of it, even to someone whose antennae were more morbidly pointed outward than mine. Nothing would have suggested there were worlds outside that world, until it was almost too late, until one almost became what one's forbears had been.

Now and then, the school would sell cheap tickets to the Cleveland Orchestra's Akron appearances or give out free ones for special programs just for kids. I never raised my hand. I never asked. My father got wind of this at school Open House.

"But you like that kind of music, don't you?"

"I guess so."

"Then why don't you ask for the tickets?"

I shrugged and said I didn't know, but the truth was, I simply thought I wasn't allowed. I thought the kids who were allowed to go to the symphony had been told that on the first day of class, and it was they who raised their hands for the tickets. Not us. Not me. Years later when it is time to pick a college, I do not even consider the Ivy League or some big school out of state. *I think it isn't allowed. I think it's not for me. I assume they will laugh.*

That Goodyear Heights was a tough neighborhood didn't occur to me until we moved over to Eastwood, a neighborhood more homogenous, more suburban and safe, where I found myself regarded as a tough interloper. We'd always compared ourselves to the kids from Seiberling School, who were *really* tough. There were no blacks on our side of the hill, and their legendary fighting status made us think that white boys who went to school with them were a breed apart, fashioned especially to meet the mysterious circumstance of interracial contact.

We'd have been more casual with other ethnicities had we been sure of our own. At best, we were Akron's Celts, pushed to the rim, repeated defeat giving us—incredibly—an ineradicable sense of superiority. Our prefab houses clung to the steep eastern slope of the moraine, refugees pushed to the edge of the habitable environment. We skirmished strenuously, if indecisively, with the boys in the neighborhoods spread over the gentler south and west sides, where the shaded brick houses seemed huge and ancient and the streets bore names out of exotic geography, Sumatra and Malacca and Congo. It was class war, and we were the plebeians. We were smaller, younger, less honorable, little guerrillas striking hard and low against power we couldn't meet head-on.

We called each other collectively after the schools we attended, and individually after our mothers' names, a practice both universal and inexplicable. The Seiberling boys—Nancy and June and Mary and Solange—had air rifles and fathers who would chase you in defense of their sons and properties. We Betty Jane boys—Ethel and Marion and Evelyn and Leona—had only our cunning and our willingness to slink by night into enemy garages to chalk-mark the walls and stuff the barrels of air-guns with soaked sugar. We never won, exactly, but sometimes we could make their victories costly.

I saw the differences between the other Heights families and us, but I didn't think of them as invariably in our favor. Most of my approved playmates were quite violent. Our games were war and cowboys, which was war in ten-gallon hats, or Lost Civilizations, which was war in imaginary Trojan helmets. I think the violence sounded well in our parents' ears, for it was the American and Christian violence of good triumphing over evil. Hitler had been dead for less than a generation; Stalin still lived, and righteous force had acquired no taint in the nostrils of Goodyear Heights.

My friend, Ronnie, wouldn't play war. This sufficed to queer him in common conception. My other best friend, Debbie Marsh, was a pacifist too, but also a girl and so didn't count in the same way. Ronnie never spoke against violence, but he turned away when I joined in, trudging down to the creek with a bit of screen stretched between dowels to sieve among the waterweeds for insects. A measure of his quietude was, I suspect, a lack of imagination, which made the intricacies of our games partially unintelligible to him. But part of it was true and innate gentleness, the first example I ever had of such a thing. I learned to mock it with the rest.

In general, the Heights families were not lucky. They married at eighteen and, in their frenzy to keep their kids from the same mistake, drove them to the altar, or at least to the delivery room, at sixteen. Many of the nearby children were maladjusted in some way—impeded, antisocial, truant, loose-bladdered. The inside toilet was considered an option but by no means a necessity. The scent of urine mingled with flower beds and scorching asphalt.

They were the sort that went to carnivals, and, if I seemed sufficiently unenthusiastic, just politely acceding to a friend's invitation, I'd sometimes be allowed to go along. I usually had to throw up after the rides, and my carnival-going friends were good at finding places to vomit without being in the way. Throwing up was a big deal at my house, and someone held your head. But other families took it in stride, looking briefly the other way, carrying on with their conversation, growing impatient if you made a production of it.

Their daughters had assignations with carnival workers with a frequency that made me think that's why they went, to give their mothers the opportunity to bray, "... *and with a carnival barker. The scum of the earth!*" I was generally on the daughters' side, though they were too high-and-mighty fifteen to care.

People talked a good deal about background. I didn't know what ours was, really, but father and mother made it sound loftier than present circumstance. Alliance with carnivals was flatly unthinkable for anyone with our background, whatever it was. To run away with the circus or palm the third grade milk money simply did not cross my mind. I did not carry a bowie knife, like my friend Jesse. I did not light matches indoors. I did not hanker after the milkman. I had few habits that would lead me into the tribulations which seemed to be their daily fare. I admired the Heights families for their vulnerability to things that were no threat to anyone else in the world.

By some grace, my turbulence was inside. The upheavals may have been as great, but they were invisible, and I do appreciate such luck.

I wonder what story we were telling ourselves after all. What myth was Ronnie living when he turned his back on us little Rebels and paratroopers and headed for the purling creek water? What fatal princess was Linda Dietz when she let the carnival barker run his tongue along her throat under the yellow lights? What ballad did soon-to-be-divorced Mr. Schumann live when he came home from a day of trucking to a night of honky-tonk steel guitaring amid the smoke and intrigues? Our restlessness—

our energy—came in part from not knowing how we were supposed to live. We were no longer peasants, no longer wild Irish hiding in a Connemara glen, no longer gypsies rattling our wagons along a road outside some city studded with onion domes. Who were we then? We were truckers, mechanics, housewives (not one of us a poet), but that was not the same. We *did* things, but we had no unified conception of *being* anything.

Some of us, unable to find our own place in it, retreated from the Story altogether and became the dead-eyed mass that Madison Avenue postulates as the typical American, low-level Organization Men, little voids to be filled with products and services. Some of us exploded and went to jail. Of the seven families who lived in our house on Goodview Avenue from the time we left it, in 1963, until the last time I spoke with the neighbors, in 1992, four had dispersed because of trouble with the law. Some of us beat a way into the Great Story. We became teachers, engineers, poets, readers, dreamers. Circumstances at the time called for such secretiveness, though, that I cannot even tell you who they were.

If you turn your back often enough, you end up facing the way you were when you started. It is a curious fact that the people I spent so much energy escaping are the ones I feel most comfortable with now. This does not even surprise me. *Of course,* the soul says, shrugging its shoulders over and over, *you end the race with the people who were at the line when you began. Why did I even bother to fight?*

Perhaps the answer is, *to hold that place.*

3 . THE QUEEN OF THE COWGIRLS

Mercy on me, Spirit,

> *for the fierce lucidity,*
> *the stuff of poetry, but the man-destroyer,*
> *the fender-off of hearts;*
> *for the charity almost never withheld*
> *but sometimes crammed down the wrong throat,*
> *a feast for the merely peckish,*
> *the starving left with a high smile and a poem,*
> *prostrate at the roadside.*

THAT DEBBIE MARSH came from a broken home was a fact as widely distributed as it was unacknowledged. It's not that separation, even divorce, was such a horror in our neighborhood, lower middle class and amorously liquid. It was the circumstance of it. Her father left her mother not for another woman, but for a man.

Information such as this is not intrinsically shocking to seven-year-olds. We knew that Mr. Marsh had gone to live with his boyfriend. We had seen the boyfriend sitting in the car while Mr. Marsh got some things from the house. But when the story was told officially, we concluded we had gotten something wrong. It didn't sound like what we had seen. My mother did not say, "Mr. Marsh has gone to live with his friend." She drooped her hand at the wrist, pursed her lips, and went into an act so odd I recognized neither it nor her. "Mr. Marsh is *strange*. It's not right that he should be around here any more. If he comes near you or touches you, come and tell Mommy immediately."

"What's strange about him?"

"What do you mean?"

"You said Mr. Marsh was strange."

"Don't you worry about that. You just do what I told you."

I did worry about it, especially about what would happen if Mr. Marsh touched me. Would I be "strange," too? Would my wrist and my lips go as my mother's had gone when she talked about him? Mother told me a lot of things: don't touch this, please do that, come when I call. But the way she talked about Mr. Marsh was different, with an urgency, or perhaps a glee, that was uncommon from her.

I saw Mr. Marsh several times later. He looked the same, maybe a little happier, surviving in memory in the image of the young Walter Brennan. What was "strange" about him remained obscure. I think he would have told me had I the courage to ask, though perhaps the answer would still not have made sense. In our own world at the time, the difference between playing with girls and playing with boys was slight and without moral weight. We wouldn't have been able to credit that it made that much difference among adults.

Mrs. Marsh's name was Gladys. "Gladys" sounded like something falling down, like the report of a rifle or the shattering of a stone wall. Perhaps I associated it with "collapse." Gladys was nothing like that, nothing dangerous or epic. If I met her now, I would probably think of her as one of those good old gals with whom playwrights populate Southern beauty shops. She had hair bleached white. I got to watch her bleach it once when I was there and her beautician friend came over. Gladys and her friend talked about men and smoked cigarettes. They asked me which lipstick color I liked, and I liked the brightest red. They turned to me when the conversation needed a man's perspective, and that was thrilling. They were *women* not my mother, and they were relating to *me,* and that was most thrilling of all.

Gladys was an object of sympathy to my mother and the other neighbors because of her "troubles," but I thought her jolly, like an aunt that you saw often enough for friendly relations but not so often as to be a nuisance. She was the last person you'd figure would be married to anyone strange in any way. Gladys had "headaches" that I now recognize as alcoholic binges. On those days, her children were sent to play at our house.

The Marshes lived two doors down in a house nearly identical to ours. Both Mr. Marsh and my father worked at Goodyear, and everyone else we knew, except the beauticians, had jobs that were somehow related to rubber.

The daughter of this pair was Debbie Marsh, and she was my best friend. Though active, even aggressive, in many ways, I tend to be passive in affairs of the heart, waiting to be sought out and courted. Debbie Marsh sought me out and courted me in a manner I still think of as a model of straightforwardness. There were no boys to play with, and would be none until I was old enough to wander down toward Adelaide Hill, or when I went to school and met some there. For two years or so, we were each other's total social world. There was nothing we could not say to each other. If I heard her speaking now, I might remember her, for, after more than thirty years apart, there are ways in which I know Debbie Marsh better than anyone else on earth. Of course, I picture her frozen in a moment of time, but do we not picture ourselves the same? I became who I am when I was nine years old. Anyone who knew me at that instant would know me now. I think Debbie Marsh was Debbie Marsh even before that.

She had a belt made of gold coins set in plastic. The profiles on the gold coins were austere and classical. We decided they were presidents who lived before Washington, who no longer counted because they lost the war. I remember her standing on a mound of dirt excavated from the foundation of my father's new garage. I remember her standing in her little girl plaid dress and her belt of gold coins and announcing her plans to be a cowgirl, plans so secret she kept looking over the yard as she told them, in case some ear of one of the garage workers pointed our direction.

The term "cowgirl" is a problem in repeating the story now, though it wasn't then. We understood each other immediately and exactly. Her paradigm was Dale Evans, "Queen of the Cowgirls", spouse of Roy Rogers, "King of the Cowboys." The idea of kings and queens was the significant part, not the particular people who bore the titles. A child's mind, as I have said, is allegorical. So many things are not what they first appear to be, so much lies disguised behind misleading adult explanations that one begins to assume all visible things are masks before some hidden reality. The mixing of royal and western terminology signaled to us that what the Queen of the Cowgirls and the King of the Cowboys ruled was a land away to the west where you wore deep fringes on your shirt, where you rode your own water-colored horse, and where—above all—you were at once sovereign and free. To be a king or queen was to rule over yourself.

A psychologist might say that Debbie was signaling her need for control over her life, and that would probably be true. Possibly we were aware of that then, but also that the immediate applications were only a fragment of a beautiful story.

The *Iliad* is a tale about hurt feelings, and its participants might even have known that, but they would never have *settled* for it. The hurt feelings would have to fill the space between heaven and earth. Debbie's word "cowgirl" invoked a world to which the two TV syllables were merely a key. She would be Queen of the Cowgirls, and I would be King of the Cowboys, and between us no further explanation was necessary. We would be monarchs in our own land, sunset-ridden, leaping with dangerous animals, unbounded by the rules that keep the ordinary world gray and predictable. Of all humans, it would include just us two.

Debbie chose me when she could have been playing with doll-dressing tea-party-giving Susan Perolio two doors up. It was more the selection of a compatible imagination than of a playmate. I chose her when I could have been running the solitary epics of my imagination.

Our favored pastime was the Blue Story. To begin the Blue Story, one of us related a tale we'd heard or made up. In the process of the narration, a strange thing happened: we stopped recounting and *became*. We were not pretending. We were transformed. It was like those dreams in which you remain fully involved with the experience and yet know you dream, inhabiting and savoring the moment at once. Any good story telling has an aspect of transformation, but some energy Debbie and I generated together lifted us beyond the suspension of disbelief into pure identity. The Blue Story was like a vehicle that didn't move but folded space and time around itself and condensed all moments into a sphere. A particular sensation had simply to be reached for to be lived.

Sometimes the agent of this transformation would be Debbie's collection of dolls in national dress. She chose a doll dressed in green shamrocked silk or a Highland tartan or a flamenco dancer's bright fountainy skirt, and we concentrated until we achieved the moment called "Blue."

Blue is hard to explain. It had something to do with the color blue, how it appears behind closed eyes as though you have a sky inside that materializes when you're thinking of nothing in particular. But Blue was also a state of excited expectancy in which communication could enter from realms outside ordinary experience. The faraway came near. The holy was suddenly intimate. The once merely imagined took form. When, years later, I read "The Blue Story" in Isak Dinesen's *Winter's Tales,* I was electrified, for in that tale the same state was induced in the narrator by a piece of blue porcelain.

Blue seemed to me a species of prayer. Like "Now I Lay Me Down to Sleep," it was a magical formula, summoning unseen powers which, beyond reason, loved you and wished you to have more abundant life. Whether Debbie questioned or sought to analyze the dispensation, I don't know. I did not, beyond wondering how to bring it when we wanted, how to keep it as long as we wanted.

The dolls—like the phrase "Queen of the Cowgirls"—had no exact part in the story, but served as doors opening onto the worlds they claimed to represent. Like mediums or poets, they revealed without participating. Since we knew nothing about the Ireland or the Spain or the Wild West the dolls represented, our reveries weren't travelogues and had nothing specifically to do with the countries the dolls were meant to come from. We were like aliens deducing a world from the merest hints. That the dolls were identical beneath their costumes told us something important about the world. It told us that the surfaces of things are significant. A doll that puts on a red dancing skirt is a Spanish doll. The same doll slipped into furs and skins is an Eskimo. A god in a whale skin is a whale. In a man's, a man. Debbie Marsh and I could be who we pleased by borrowing their accouterments, by willing ourselves into their stories, as all heroes had surely done once upon a time.

During one of these sessions, it dawned on me that Mr. Marsh's defection from Goodview Avenue into the lavender haze of homosexuality had been a case of Blue. It amazed me that adults could play, too. Debbie and I had not made it up out of nothing. Then I realized why everybody was so hush-hush about Mr. Marsh's adventure, why my mother made that unmotherly face, part scorn but, I thought now, part envy. He had escaped. He had left us behind. He had become King of the Cowboys, or whatever phrase he used to translate his heart's desire. I waited for Mr. Marsh to come again, so I could look on him with my new knowledge. Of course, as in any good story, he was gone forever, the sunset sealed around him like a theater curtain.

Time passed even for Debbie and me. Gladys Marsh remarried and became Gladys Fein. Mr. Fein was a gruff giant of a man who wore blue coveralls. He added a porch to their garage, with a cement floor he painted red and on which we could ride our bikes and play Mother May I away from the dangers of the street. My mother liked him. Debbie liked him. The only person who seemed not to like him was Bobby, Debbie's younger brother. Bobby was too little most of the time to figure in our activities, and when he did, he was a brat. Mother related how Mr. Fein was having a time "beating Bobby's father out of him." I know what that means now, and how horrible the process must have been for Bobby—and how pointless—but then I got cruel pleasure out of the suffering of one whose demands sometimes came between me and his sister.

One had to be cautious around Mr. Fein, not because he was brutal but because he was sensitive and easily offended. It was obvious that one shouldn't mention his (impressive) weight, but what else there was to be offended by was not easy to tell. I saw the bottles on their coffee table, but did not know the concept, much less the word, "alcoholic." Kindred spirits had found each other.

Time brought on a horrible day. Perhaps, everything considered, and loss of innocence weighed in the balance, it was one of the four or five worst days of my life. It started out just fine. It started out as the opening of a new era. Boys my age moved into the neighborhood. As I said, I am not forward socially, and as they had yet to come courting, Debbie and I played together happily for a long while. But one day they did come. Before I was aware, we were standing in my yard talking boy talk, something I was learning on the spot. They must have noticed my unfamiliarity. Most of the cuss words I had not heard before, and used but awkwardly. I was not afraid of them, exactly, but I was confused. They wanted things from me other than what Debbie had wanted. They wanted me to *do* what Debbie and I had mostly imagined. They were at once exciting and stupid.

Debbie appeared in her backyard that day as she had day after day before. I had to look at her over the tops of the blue morning glories my father had trained into a wall between the yards. She was calling "Come over, David, come over and play." A hundred times I had heard this and had come.

They said, "You're not going to play with a girl, are you?"

Though it would have been, I see from the platform of adulthood, as easy to have said "yes," I said "no." I shouted my new cuss words over the morning glories. Debbie probably didn't understand the words any better than I, but she understood the tone. She stood and gazed silently as I played with my new pals. They would not go around to the far side of the house to play. They wanted Debbie to see the victory they were gaining over her. I would have given anything had she gone inside, but she stood watching, still as a statue.

This was the first time I betrayed anyone on purpose, and very nearly the last. This was the first time I recognized I could do wrong—real wrong, not the incomprehensible misdemeanors for which one was punished by one's parents, a sin which one recognized and lamented almost immediately, but somehow did not have the means to undo.

There's a story about a company of Zen disciples sleeping with their master around a campfire. One of the disciples awakes to feel his master beating him with a burning stick. When the beating's over, the disciple leaves off sucking his blisters for a moment to ask, "Why, master?"

"Because in a dream I perceived that the laws of karma decreed some far worse punishment in the future unless this were suffered now. I have saved you!"

My betrayal of Debbie Marsh stays with me. It probably will forever. I tell myself this trespass saved me from worse in times to come. Maybe it does, for gut-sickness afflicts me every time I think of it.

In the fullness of time, the Feins moved to Arizona. Debbie and I had reconciled by then, and I want to say "everything was as it had been before," though I have no recollection whether it was or not. I avoided self-accusation and the grief of parting by ignoring the event altogether. People moved out of our neighborhood all the time. I had new friends and didn't miss Debbie as I might have, though who those friends were I do not remember.

I would see Debbie Marsh once more. On the day before I was to go to high school, she came visiting. Her grandfather, Gladys's father, phoned at her request to set up a meeting. I resisted; Mother insisted. At a stage when I was especially ugly and awkward, Debbie was radiantly beautiful. I could barely stand to look at her, or to have her look at me. Whether she had become Queen of the Cowgirls I couldn't tell and didn't know how to ask. But she was giggly and bouncy and shed light about like any of the girls I could meet in the hall at school. I wanted to ask her about Blue, but she was so thoroughly in this world it seemed a breach of decorum to inquire about alternatives. She asked me polite questions that I answered in monosyllables, and then it was over. Mother put my shyness down to not remembering our old friendship. In that, she was quite wrong.

4 . THE TONGUE

Tell the world to trash its heap of words.
I have a syllable to start on.
N . . . N . . . that is no *and* never *and* now *and* know
I have Ah that is agony and pleasure, summon and forbid.

I FIND A PHOTOGRAPH in a box in the hall closet.
A baby sits in a highchair, a pillow at his back because he's so
small. The apartment, too, is small, and whoever is taking the
picture can't back away far enough to get everything in. The
highchair has a metal tray that can be removed for cleaning. The
baby's right hand rests on a padded chair arm. The left hand
cannot be seen. Behind are a rank of kitchen cabinets and a
chest of drawers on which sits one of those baskets covered
with gauze that people send fruit in when somebody is sick. The
line of the window is softened by a polka-dot curtain. On the
table in front of the baby is a round glass serving dish and on
the dish a birthday cake shaped like a heart. Something is written on the cake at an angle the camera does not catch. I know it
is "Happy Birthday Davie," because I know the baby is me. Out
of the cake's heart soars a single burning shaft of candle. The
baby's face is a mask of ecstasy. Whether mesmerized by the
candle or by its being his first birthday or by sheer life, he is radiant. His mouth opens in the sideways *O* of delight. The baby

is not especially beautiful, but he is happy. He focuses on the one point, the shaft of light. It all would be easier to understand if someone else were in the picture, a third point beside me and the candle in the flat walls to establish a plane. But there's just his— my—eyes and the dancing single light, the rest of the room effectively empty. Focused. Mesmerized. Delighted. The wounded adult in me wants to say, "I wish it were like that now," but the truth teller whispers, *it is like that now, often enough, and you know the reasons why.*

The reason is a merry tongue. The reason is language that can find an open door among the myriads that the gods have shut. The reason is linguistic sorcery which can find a way to transform "no" into "maybe" and "never" into "wait." Possession of such a thing is not a virtue, but almost unimaginable luck. Sometimes, in passages of futility, when to rename the agony is merely to prolong it, it represents an almost unimaginable cruelty. I do not know where it came from. I suppose a proper sign of gratitude would be to spend some moments finding out.

We all start somewhere. Would I have been a different person had I not grown up where I did? The question is untestable, but my answer is nevertheless an emphatic *yes.* There wouldn't have been the Tower Building spiking out of the downtown sleet like a vast candle anywhere else, or the Polsky's department store window filled with dolls and mechanical animals at Christmas. There wouldn't have been C. C. Harvey next door to beat me up, or the Soap Box Derby to give me twelve years of mortification because I was unmechanical, or the ragged hillside woods to make me love the wilderness of which they were a ragged and imperiled remnant.

From Trieste, James Joyce allowed his mind to wander the streets of his native Dublin. He needed to get away from the brawling home place to write, but he needed to return, in spirit at least, in order to possess what he needed to write about. His waking life was elsewhere, but his story was still *there,* where he was born, among the people who knew him at his best and worst, among the people who spoke his language so intimately and effortlessly that he would never understand anybody as perfectly as he understood them. Nor—whether this is a paradox or a truism I don't know—would he ever be misunderstood by any as diligently as he would be by them.

I wondered if one could do this with Akron, which, if a hundred writers took a hundred years to glorify it, could not have the glamour of Joyce's city on the Liffey, not because of something in itself, but because that's not what the imagination allows for Midwestern towns looming up out of the farms like rawboned boys. I could, of course, follow its streets as they were in memory, but I wouldn't know to where, or what I would be seeking, or whose voice would be my voice in the narrative. I've lived elsewhere for twenty years. I've lost track of the dramas that unfold behind those familiar facades. I didn't know them when I lived there, either, because then I didn't care. The world that mattered was somewhere else. I assumed there were no dramas, no passions, none of the glamour in Akron which I read about in books. I assumed that I would have to get as far away as possible, as soon as possible, to have the life I imagined for myself. And because it was thus imagined, it was true.

I was a poet. I had been a poet since before I knew what a poem was. I had been one since my grandmother recited Tennyson and Whittier to me in the shade under her apple trees, and I hadn't known they were poems, only that they were electrifying and strange and far enough from my daily world to constitute a world I wanted. To be able to say, "I am a poet," knocked me from my place in east Akron, where you could perhaps *be* such a creature but never *say* it. If it gave me place elsewhere, it has taken a lifetime to discover where.

I was a *real* poet from the very first, on the basis of a quality of perception, innate and difficult to describe. I became a *bad* poet when I went to a summer school for the gifted at East High and learned actually how to write a poem. ABAB. Quatrain. Classical allusion. Something about nature or memory. God, I was good at it! Given a pattern like that, an obsessive like me can turn out epics in a summer night. How Miss Niehoff praised me! How I was shown to visiting dignitaries as a prodigy to be!

> . . . and if I could have one wish at all
> I'd wish for a cottage by a cool waterfall.

. . . except I wouldn't, really, not then and not now. Nor was I fooled by my own facility. It was part of a game. I was waiting for something to come, some great theme that couldn't be tossed off in a minute or two, my brain calculating the effect on my beloved teacher, scanning my classmates for that delicious exhalation, envy. I wanted those things, but I was not fooled by them. They would do until the real vision, whatever it was, came along.

Facility is a form of camouflage. Do a vivid thing easily, with flash and verve, and people are satisfied with you and let you alone. Then, in deep cover, you can go about the real work.

In callow youth, I believed I was the only boy from Akron who'd ever wanted to be a poet. I believed that, a poet, I had been dropped into a uniquely unpoetic environment, and that Fate had done this as a gesture of mercy, to allow me to go about my development unobserved, like a prince in hiding, secure in rags and dirt from the eyes of enemies. Serious conversation about poetry was impossible because one didn't know anybody who wanted to talk about it, nor even anybody to ask where to find such a person. Merely to ask was to open oneself up to ridicule, or what was worse, the clucking attention of adults who thought that such a desire was public property, theirs to praise and encourage in the most sickening manner, theirs to call on to perform at assemblies and Honors Day programs, where the humiliation of being noticed as a *scholar* was bad enough, let alone a *poet*.

If I had just been the fastest runner at Hyre Junior High, or the meatiest linebacker, there would have been a context for me. I knew there was nothing equivalent for what I was, so I didn't ask for one, but I kept watching. Being a poet in such a place and time is a little like being a homosexual. At first you imagine there is nobody in the world like you. Then there are hints and whispers, the odd figure stopping in the alley pointing to himself and then at you: *you, too?* After a while, you know at a glance who is and who isn't.

Back before they built the Wedgewood Acme Click, the street opposite the junior high leaned up against an extensive urban woods. The path leading into the woods lay opposite the windows of Mr. Graham's biology room, and, every morning early, a woman in slacks and sweatshirt could be seen entering the greenwood by that path. "That's Mrs. So-and-so," one of my classmates whispered, "So-and-so's mother. She's a *poet*. She goes in there to *write poems.*" The tone is impossible to reproduce in print, but it implied wonder, prodigy, and disapproval all at once, the unspoken subtext being, "while everybody else's mother is home keeping house or out adding to the income." I was electrified. It was as though a paleontologist had been pointed toward a live dinosaur. I had no idea how to meet that woman. Rushing from the biology class was, then, unthinkable. It didn't even occur to me to get her number from her daughter and call her on the phone. Such direct approaches to the things you desired—unless what you desired was very ordinary—were not thought of. Nevertheless, she made an indelible impression, creeping into the shadows like that, as though she, too, were hiding, as though my impulse to secrecy had been right from the start.

No one would know I aimed at Parnassus. It would never

cross anybody's mind that anyone in such a place as that would have such an ambition. I believed this even after I saw Mrs. So-and-so sneaking into the woods, for she was clearly an anomaly, furtive and possibly ashamed. I believed this until I read Hart Crane, who, coming out of Garrettsville, thought of Akron as a metropolis boiling with imaginative possibilities. I believed it until I mentioned Hart Crane to my mother, thinking to terrify her with legends of monsters in the town she had innocently inhabited all her life, and she won the match by saying, "Oh, Hart. I knew him. Used to buy candy from him—where was it? Schumacher's? Down on Mill Street. He was a strange boy."

Dumbfounded, I tried to recover the initiative. "Did you know he was a famous poet?"

"Was he? That would explain a lot."

What? What did it explain? I couldn't ask, for that would blow my cover. I looked at my mother with curiosity. *She had known him. She had known a poet and had not been in awe. She hadn't even noticed. If she knew it about me, would that, too, explain a lot?*

I thought I was the only boy in Akron who ever wanted to be a poet, until I went to college and met Ralph La Charity, a kid from away East somewhere, who confided to me that he had given up on school a year before in order to hang out on the streets of the most poetical city in America, where "the Tongue," the essential American speech, was still spoken with verve and purity. "If you want to be a poet, man, that's where you have to go. Not school. Can't learn the Tongue in school."

Oh, I wanted to be a poet. I wanted the Tongue with my whole soul. "Where?" I asked anxiously. "What city is it?"

"Akron, man, Akron, Ohio. It's the capital of the Tongue."

Ralph and Mother united in ghostly alliance. I had heard the Tongue of Poets all my life and had not even noticed. Mother had bought chocolates from the wildest of them and had not thought it worth mentioning. I had been speaking the

Tongue all along. *Listen to this, ladies, and gentlemen, it is the Tongue!* The perfect long vowels. The emphatic *R*. The accentless efficiency, like a sharp blade cutting metal in a factory. Perhaps I had been born in a place that was poetical after all, but hid it under a screen of rubber smoke against the mockery and suspicion of the world. Akron was a grungy kid who worked hard in the rubber plants by day, crept home at night and, still dirty, still exhausted, while his folks watched TV at the other end of the hall, locked himself in his room, writing poems by the dim light of a covered lamp.

And the kid still does this even when he realizes that he will lose everything else. Otherwise, it was just a phase. A poet is a poet because he wants to be something *more,* more than to be a kid from Goodyear Heights, more than to be a geek with glasses on the sidelines of the Big Game, more than he knows how to be. It is a Faustian endeavor. You must go out of yourself to have it, and then there's no guarantee than you can get your old self back. And years later, when you realize it was just fine to be a kid from Goodyear Heights, just fine to be the happy kid with the glasses on the sidelines, you wonder why you bothered.

Still, the first and last rule of life is Transformation. Nobody history cares about stood still. The preliminary form of Transformation is Sacrifice. None of us is born as we should be. Mothers and fathers sacrifice for us because they love us from near at hand; poets sacrifice for us because they love us from afar, or because they are in love with poetry, the instrument of Transformation. The poet is willing to be the all-day catalyst, to burn in the fire that will refine not himself but others.

Yet, like Yahweh, one also is the I Am, the fully achieved, the Dweller in the Moment. To be That Which Transforms and That Which Stands Still at the same time only seems a paradox. Think for a moment of a high jumper caught midair in a photograph. He is beautiful in the frozen instant, his form perfect, the history of the leap evident in his posture and position and the determined expression of his face. Yet we would misinterpret the image utterly were we ignorant that the point of it was movement. Whatever perfection his image has in the photo is changed to another perfection in the ensuing nanosecond, and yet remains perfect. The world we stand on moves and remains at apparent rest, and is yet one world. The only fatal mistake which can be made—and the one perpetual in the "revealed" religions such as Christianity and Economics—is to stop creation where creation itself has not stopped.

My habit of equating the artist with the god shocks even me. All you have to do is know a few artists to know how equivocal you should feel about that comparison, and yet what I mean is simply that their modes of operation are the same. God and Shakespeare were reading from the same manual. Each work of art is a finished artifact, the perfect expression of the moment— the high jumper caught in the instant—and yet the artist has already moved on from that moment to achieve a different perfection, or perhaps to ease into extinction. Like a god, the artist moves without assurance that he will be able to make his creation move along with him. God fills the dirt with fossils; the poet his desk with outgrown poems.

The sun sinks under North Hill, spraying the Cuyahoga with copper light. The plumes from the stacks of the rubber plants turn pink and gold, spreading into low clouds, beautiful if you didn't know what they were, if you had no sense of smell. People hurry to get home, to sit down to their suppers, everyone speaking at once, telling the stories of their days. The smells of garlic and Mediterranean sauces rise from north Akron; cheap beef, beer, potatoes from the east; delicate spices and French wines from the rich folks over on the west; soul food and the omnipresent taint of rubber in the center and the south. Summit Lake goes up in cool fire. A few boats light out from shore, the rower and the passenger stopping in the middle of the golden water for an entwining of arms, a meeting of lip on lip. Under Main Street, the canal runs on in darkness, bearing air, interrupted by shafts of red and gold from the broken pavement: the city hiding its first life, the canal and the bargemen and the runaway slaves, with its second, the factories and department stores and the derelicts sitting on the stoop of the Hotel Anthony Wayne for a last glimpse of evening light. If asked where they come from, they'll all say it with a note of apology. Nobody important comes from *there*. Or if they do, they're not saying. Keep the secret. Let them go their way undetected.

In the Goodyear Heights Metropolitan Park, the raccoons wake to forage, the lights of the neighborhoods twinkling through the branches.

Under the mysterious surface of Blue Pond, the drowned dancers keep on dancing.

Where did you become a poet?

Home. Because it was the least likely place imaginable.

Why did you become a poet?

Because I had no other choice.

Why do you continue?

To have my way.

To make someone love me who first loved my words.

To beat into the undiscovered country.

To sing to sleep the Angel at the burning Gate, and so sneak past.

Because I was born with a bird where my brain should be. I took that for a sign.

Because, in my wildest moments, I have cherished the Word as the one weapon against God.

5. AMONG WARRIORS

Like a minor god in an epic—absurd but memorable—
I come howling prophecies of our future,
bearing our history before me like bronze armor
useless equally for affront or defense,
the prop of an old heroic play
to which the script is lost.

SOME USE LIBRARIES to discover the way things are. I used them for raw materials to form a world that was not, yet in imagination ought to be. A library was indistinguishable from a forest or a creekbed, in that it provided pure information, objective, delicious, jumbled, material I could order toward the formation of a world. I used the library to discover more cunning, more spectacular means of conquest.

In the library, as in the midst of any fantasy, I chose the most vivid of available possibilities, which were often also the bloodiest. On the playing fields, in the moonlit streets, in the schoolyard, conflict loomed in the imagination of our childhood. It has been a harsh century. Nobody we knew remembered peace. Maybe that's why.

The poet should not ignore the uses of catastrophe. It is the great shortcut, the jump-start that gets the engines moving when philosophies and political systems bog down. I do not recommend; I merely observe. Robinson Jeffers suggests that violence is the sire of all our values; I'd finished graduate school before it occurred to me to think of that statement as ironic. Left to our own devices, we boys played Civil War or Iwo Jima. Playground snow forts were not merely architectural projects, but the Walls of Troy from which we sallied with a clash of imagined bronze. All children are bloody-minded. A trip to the toy store confirms this. It is well, though. It is a phase that must be gotten over by going through. Parents who deny their children toy guns witness the transformation of all other vaguely linear objects—sticks, boards, pencils—into blasters or magnums by force of imagination. We were born fighting the cave bear, and something in us retains that energy to this hour.

It was an attitude our elders did not discourage. For many in my mother's generation, World War II, with its shared dangers and unity of purpose, was the most wonderful of memories, so keen and present that under their influence I grew up thinking that "the War" was a perpetual state, a locality more than an event. One could visit the War and witness danger and heroism firsthand. I had dreams about "Going to the War," in which it was found through an extension of the house, a long corridor one followed until one heard bullets. Grandpa gave me a book of ration stamps and adventure novels whose covers boasted that they were made of the worst paper, to conserve the best for the war effort. Uncle Walter gave me a coloring book of World War II aircraft, virgin, new, printed on that rough brown stock they had to use. Uncle Richard still had his leather jacket from Korea, with a dragon rampant on the back.

Saturday war movies at the Linda Theater on Goodyear Boulevard intensified this impression. Where else could they have been filmed but at the War? We dreamed of war, not wicked dreams, but heroic ones that inspired the exultation sexual dreams would inspire a few years further on. Our enemies at play were still Japs and Krauts. Commies never replaced them in the bloodier passages of juvenile imagination. I believe this is because the atom bomb taught even children something about uncritical enthusiasm in war. Never again do we dare hate an enemy so purely. Though it is a hard thing to say, the Germans and the Japanese as enemies arise from a time of innocence. Things will never be so uncomplicated again. The War can never be kept so far distant, so "over there" again. There is no more "over there."

In any event, there was dislocation in learning that this great moment, the War of the World, the last righteous combat, had been over for ten years. It created a void not wholly filled by Korea, which did not possess the unambiguousness necessary to the heroic.

John Ruskin made the observation that the art which we cherish all arises from warrior nations. By this he meant his own England, of course, and beloved Greece, but it is worth considering as a general observation. Energy is energy. Shakespeare rises from the life throes of adolescent England, Bach over the rubble of the Thirty Years War. The problematic phrase in Ruskin is, of course, "which we cherish." We cherish the heroic, the struggle, whether successful or not. Young writers are told to include and accentuate conflict in their stories. I do not know whether this is a universal human impulse or a cultural habit, but I know it is strong in me, and I would not have it otherwise. Mystics reach God with the vocabulary of rape, poets with the language of the battlefield. Surely, in motionless times, in mean times, a poet should not fear invocation of the demons of strife.

One further thing to be said for war play is this: I wonder if I would have learned how to be loyal, how to take on large, perhaps dangerous responsibility without it. I wonder if, lacking a physical image of it, I would have discovered in good time who I am? We are accustomed in nature documentaries to hearing that the play of fox kits and lion cubs is preparation for the work of life, the building of muscles, the setting of reflexes, the determination of social order. The same thing is true for the man-cub. When we played Civil War, Jesse was always was a Reb, I always a Yank. I couldn't see the point of deliberately choosing the losing side; Jesse couldn't imagine a situation in which he would not be the Byronic loser, going down with guns blazing. One of us was inevitably the oldest brother in our brothers' band of warriors, one inevitably the youngest. Some shrugged and took whatever role was assigned to them. One of us was going to be wounded; one of us was going to fix him up. The casting was all but invariable, though new roles and new plots could be added if a new TV show or movie captured our imagination. All the while I was learning, without the intrusion of a classroom or an adult, who I was and what I was good at. I was learning from the other boys what was expected of me in a cooperative situation. I am not by nature much of a joiner, and what the other boys knew about working together, a knowledge which seemed effortless and innate, did not cease to amaze me.

The annihilation of the other side was never an issue, for we were typically all on the same side and the adversary—Krauts or spacemen or, if we were animals that time, hunters—remained purely imaginary. Even the game of Rebs and Yanks involved one or the other of us (Jesse, usually) coming home wounded and being reconciled to the brothers who clove to the other side.

When an innovation came to the play, it nearly always sprung from my omnivorous, unselective reading habits. No combination was too preposterous, no situation too grandiose. I peopled Dodge City with dinosaurs. It was I who added Aztec Warriors (our invisible opponents being the Spaniards), Greeks and Trojans (nearly all of us wanted to be Trojans, so we could be inside the fort), and at one point Gods and Titans. What on earth could an eavesdropping adult have imagined, hearing Jesse Franklin, the neighborhood bad boy, screaming, "Die, Briarius!" hurling his invisible thunderbolts. At one point, I even convinced the crew that World War II Platoon in the Pacific needed a library, and that I was the librarian, and when they were wounded or tuckered out, I'd suggest some good reading for their recovery time. It is mortifying to think on, but then there was no evident judgment. Everything was possible. Everything was tinder for our imaginations. That one's later life should have a note of chaos in it is less surprising when one's youth was so free of boundaries, so abundant in the rewards of speculation.

Jesse, the one always blamed and the one usually at fault, the wounded Reb, tangled with authority—eventually the law itself—several times before we left high school. I became a mythologizer, a poet. I haven't kept up with the rest enough to know what became of them, but I'd bet none of it, after those intense afternoons together, would be a surprise.

I was physically the youngest of our group, and perhaps that is why I was the last to grow out of the imagined war games; indeed, I have not quite grown out of them at all. Jesse (until axed for fighting), Jack, Ronnie, Ricky, all trooped off to Little League—which I suppose was a more sanctioned version of what we'd been doing all along—while I stood at the edge of the yard watching, abandoned and forlorn, inventing epics that one could perform alone. *One of the things you're never supposed to do is leave your buddy,* I wanted to call after them, the Basic Lesson, taught first because it was the foundation of all. But time had changed. New rules were in effect.

❋

In the old argument between nature and nurture, heredity and environment, I come down heavily on the side of nature. I remember learning things, of course, and changing the way I behave, but I cannot remember being a different person than I am, and my memory is both long and precise. Events have turned in such a way that I am no longer in contact with the friends of my extreme youth, but I would like to find them again, to test this, to see if I would really know what they were going to do in a given situation, if I could hand them a script saying "Reb" or "Eldest" on the cover and watch them slip seamlessly in.

My imagination is violent. I excuse this by declaring that my imagination is violent that my deeds might not be. Whether this is a mendacity I don't know. What I do know is that energy is energy, and that the storm that shatters the coastline is the storm that seeds the forests, and that I cannot distinguish the violence of anger in me from the violence of creation, until I have witnessed the outcome.

6 . MOTHERLAND

In this season everything turns into a lady,
the rain trailing its loose hems,
the round land swollen with intent.
I am the lone man walking the mother mist,
beating the swirls of it away around me,
the one bass of the chorus,
son and brother,
father and lover,
erect in the aching sweet horizontal of spring.

SUMMER EVENINGS in my home in the Smokies, I
hike the old logging roads that rise from Bent Creek. I go at
evening because that's the time to see box turtles. The turtles dig
themselves to the shell rim into the loose dirt of the roads, to
have its radiant heat around them as deep into night as possible.
I can count on seeing three or four, probably the same ones each
time. I pat their shells as I pass, saying, "Blessings, ancient one."
This is a ritual I insist is necessary, though I am well aware I
made it up. Why should this ritual be different from the rest of
my life? From my ancestors—who might have been druids,
kings, corsairs—I have inherited exactly nothing. Everything
must be invented from the ground up.

The turtles' aspect is feminine and changeless. That some of them bear the brighter shells of males is insignificant. It is difficult to get them out of my mind after an evening jog along Bent Creek. They are goddesses, of course, presiding spirits of patience and eternity. The world balances on their great-grandmother's back.

In this age of instant sensation, anything powerful enough to shock me earns a subsequent period of deep reflection.

The design of the shield of Achilles in the *Iliad* shocks me for daring and vision notable even in the labor of a god, a whole world and the cycle of seasons encompassed in a circle of gold. Dante's discovery that mortal love is a type and road map of divine love shocks me, that a thing should be at once so beautiful and so lucky. Keats's assertion, in the "Bright Star" sonnet, that it is one's right to insist on eternity and carnality in a single ecstatic moment shocks me. The adagio of Beethoven's A minor quartet shocks me, that human creation can be at once transcendent and, in the ordinary sense of the word, meaningless. That the elements in my body have come from the throes of variously expiring stars shocks me speechless.

What shocked me once, and still continues to do so through a barrage of skeptics and revisionists, is the "Eve hypothesis." The Eve hypothesis suggests that human mitochondrial DNA can, conceivably, be traced back to a single individual African woman alive a quarter of a million years ago. Mitochondria are tiny power packs within each cell: retorts, as it were, of the chemistry of the life process. Some scientists think the mitochondria may be internal strangers, originally separate organisms, now housed in us by a symbiotic arrangement as old as multicellular life. Every cell of every body has them, and their DNA, their genetic code, is a donation exclusively from our mothers. The fire within the fire is feminine.

Divert yourself sometime by imagining the ancients possessed of modern scientific technology: Ptolemy with a two-hundred-inch reflector telescope, Aristotle with an electron microscope. Had the female heritage of mitochondrial DNA been known to Aquinas, he might have declared them to be the vessels of Original Sin, little bullets of despair passed eternally down from Eve. He'd have the physical operation basically right, though the metaphysical assumptions remain untestable. Milton might have thought them the encoded voice of the fallen archangel, crumpled, hidden, repetitious, a letter memorized because too terrible to read.

The fact of this legacy from our mothers is astonishing enough; that it all should have passed through the genetic matrix of a single historical woman is almost too much to contemplate. It is science imitating myth. Still, we have known Eve in our blood forever; confirmation of her by science is at once welcome and presumptuous.

This single woman was not, of course, utterly alone in a human population that even then must have equaled that of a Midwestern county seat. If Eve was somewhat as we supposed, Eden was not. Picture a moonlit plain gleaming with the eyes of predators. It was a tough time. There were many casualties. Some women bore only sons. Eve bore at least one daughter, and through her the world.

Whatever the circumstances, she is the Chosen Progenitrix. The Vessel, the Mother of the World. Time's Beloved.

Mother.

Whether she was paired with a single Father Adam is presently unknowable, and irrelevant.

Given the power to recede in time and lay eyes on any one person, I'd choose this Eve. I'd crouch on the savannah, watching, trying to find myself in her gestures, in the ruffles of her voice, in the widening of her eyes when she peers toward the rising moon. I'd plumb her for my ten billion brothers, my ten billion sisters who learned their marrow and their blood from her.

I'd try to tell her of her children. "All will be well," I'd say, thinking as I said it that it may turn out to be the truth.

She'd answer, "I know," and go on her way beneath the moonlight.

Of course, Mother Eve had a mother, but if we recede in time, and recede again, we must of logical necessity come to a moment when the mother was not fully human, though the daughter was. I want to see this pair. I want to be able to watch them, to know, at the one instant when it was possible to know, the division between the little Us and the enormous Them.

Before we were, before Mother Eve was, there was Mother the Forest.

Since the retreat of the glaciers—in some places, long before—trees began a mile inland from the Atlantic, suffered temporary interruption at the crest of the Alleghenies and at the Mississippi, flagged at the edge of a desert of grass. A thousand miles of oak. Maple. Chestnut. Sassafras. Beech. Dogwood. The wounds of the cherries clustered with bees. Oak crowns quivered in the distance with the scratching of bears. The tulips held their green-gold goblets of flower against the moon. Maiasaurs shredded the leaves and berries of the dogwood to feed their broods before there was grass to make the plains. This was a forest so vast that Europeans, used to the tilled fields and open landscapes of their homes, went mad crossing it. They dropped their gear and wandered in distraction. Men cried out like animals and lost themselves in the tossing shadows. The maniac scream of the pileated woodpecker remembers them.

Like shipwrecked sailors, they drank in the light at storm tears in the canopy. Those who could afford the easy way went down the rivers, daylight following like a white snake over their heads. Mother's great-aunt Ruth spoke of the shock of walking onto the banks of the Monongahela after living the first twelve years of her life under trees. Light. Space. It was high summer, and yet she could see the moon rise like a broken cup in the east. Her family couldn't pull her from the riverbank. They did their business in town and came back for her, bringing a ten-cent spyglass so she could look at things across the river. She looked, and looked, never in her life having seen farther than she could toss an apple core.

Aunt Ruth was eighty and blind when I knew her. She would not part with the spyglass regardless of her eyes and though one asked ever so politely.

In some rare and dwindling places where neither glacier nor logger reached, there are trees so old and huge they seem part of a separate creation. Joyce Kilmer Forest near the western tip of North Carolina is one such. It escaped the glaciers. Its groves are incalculably old. Its mountain species ride the eroding cliffs down as the warmth of the present interglacial lures the valley species up. They meet, mingle, strangle, and ascend. In the East, you are not likely to see larger trees. The tulips, *Liriodendron tulipifera,* rise sixty feet before sending out limbs thick as ordinary forest trees. *Liriodendron* is a sort of supermagnolia, and late in spring puts forth sturdy green and orange flowers high in her crown, which, in the winds of succeeding weeks, she sends crashing to the ground at some peril, I suppose, to smaller forest fauna. The fragrance of these airy flowers is not tulip-like at all, not even magnolia-like, but clean, subtle, a little musky, a morning scent after a perfumed night. It is a scent the dinosaurs knew. The browsing teeth of the thunder lizards drove the tulip's leaves into midheaven. Like the crocodile and the whale, *Liriodendron* has nothing to fear now from anything once it passes its adolescence. Except, of course, from us.

What fascinates still more is that there was life before there were the trees, and some of it is still there. What is it like to be a creature who can say to the towering tulips, the ancient-past-imagining magnolias, *Welcome, child, I remember the world that was before you were?* The tortoises can say this.

The tortoises lumber, browse, drowse in the slant sun coming at last under the limbs.

Deep summer. A deer holds up one hoof, peers over her shoulder to look. She calculates the energy needed to run and decides to stand still. She's safe. It's just me, running Bent Creek in the milky light of summer. Rains have been good this year. The creek and the river it feeds are swollen, the yellow and purple flowers riotous, the mosquitos abundant. Somehow the dust is immortal even after rain. Dust coats the road while the woods gleam with moisture. Dust gilds the leaves and weathered trunks. Dust flies from the wheels of passing pickups. Dust eddies in a backwash of Bent Creek like handfuls of scattered gold. Birds in the dusty branches taunt me, knowing I leave my glasses in the car when I run and cannot see them. The creek runs below like a companion who cannot quite keep up, yet who will be there, singing, to meet me at the end. Human lovers cling together down in the thickets, their radios blaring, the oily sweetness of their campfires joining the smell of dust and forest on the hill path. Their heads swivel as I pass, swivel back to the matter at hand.

At the roadside, I find the shattered shell of a box turtle. The sheath sloughs as I touch it, exposing the white bone below, four molded panels joined by jagged seams like stitches in an ivory cloth. I know what turtle this was, and that she must have been killed deliberately, and by men. No animal around here is capable of shattering a turtle shell. I pick up the fourfold shield, stuff it in my pocket for remembrance, for luck, maybe, if I don't consider what kind. I run on. I assume I will not think of it again.

Half a mile later I stop, bend over with my hands against my belly, burst into tears.

Something has unbalanced me. *O mother,* I hear my bones cry into the dust, *forgive.*

My mother was born in Akron. She had two brothers. In old photographs, she's blonde and full faced, though by the time she reached adolescence her hair had darkened to deep brown. When it's cut straight across, she looks like Buster Brown. She holds her cat in her lap, an old stray called Randy-cat. Sometimes Randy-cat is dressed in doll clothes, his gaze shot into the upper distance, loftily refusing to acknowledge the humiliation. The light in the pictures is always leafy and dappled, as though she lived in a garden. An orchard comes closer to the facts—apples, cherries, plums, creeping moonflowers. In the last picture in her back-home album, she holds a baby in the shade of a plum tree, the leafy dapple thrown on a stuccoed plane I know to be the wall of her father's garage. The baby is me.

I am trying to remember what she said about her childhood. Much of it withered away in illnesses, much more in the idle convalescence medical wisdom thought necessary back then. But was it happy? If she told me, I can't recall.

If not happy, part of it was at least magical. A few details descend: Summers in the Pennsylvania mountains of her father's people, the local shape-changers gathering vervain by Bald Eagle Creek so they could run by night in the bodies of wildcats and foxes and the long-legged birds of the lowlands; Great Aunt Pearl and her motorcycle lover, the delicate doll's tea set left behind when cycle and lover and Aunt Pearl flew from the brink of Moshannon Mountain. Pearl was not yet twenty when she died, forever young and, by the photographs, beautiful; comparing her with the ancient great-aunts, her sisters, who told the story, gave me a glimpse of the withering power of time.

Mother's mountain cousins were eccentric even in that unconventional milieu. The rumor was that one had borne a litter of puppies to the Devil, who came to her in the shape of a great black dog. Catching my mother's intense gaze, the cousin said, "You're dying to ask, aren't you?" The cousin's reticence or Mother's sense of drama never let the answer be revealed.

There are a handful of photographs from the 1940s, taken during Mother's trip with a friend to Detroit. They were working girls, and each wore a long muskrat coat and the full hair and lipsticked Cupid's bow lips of an Andrews sister. The gleam of their youth shines out of pictures now fifty years old. Though I know she never drank, she looks drunk, nevertheless, on the joy of being twenty and footloose with a pal in a distant city. I try to imagine knowing her before I was born. Was she seductive? Was she a tease? Boy crazy? Serious? Pensive? From the photos, I would say that "bashful" was not even a possibility. That one's mother might have been—by all evidence was—a *femme fatale* is a bit of information impossible fully to digest.

One time, I walked into her room as she was going through old boxes pulled from a larger wooden box in the closet. She held in her hand a chest full of beautiful silk scarves, many of them embroidered with messages, such as, "To Marion, with all my love" and "I'll be seeing you in all the old familiar places" and "Toots!" I'd seen it before she could hide it away, and when I asked what it was, she told me, reluctantly at first, but later with the warmth of remembrance, that these were gifts from boys that she met, who then went overseas to the war, to Saipan and Okinawa and Omaha Beach. When they asked her what she wanted them to send her, she always said, "a scarf," and there they were, a dozen, a score, more. She took out six. Those were the ones who did not come back.

The sight of those scarves was a little embarrassing at the time. I was not ready for the truth that my mother had once a vivid and eventful life, and that I, in fact, may have helped to put that to an end. But I have thought of them later with a much different attitude. I know what she was doing kneeling by her closet with the scarf box in her hand. She was giving those boys new life. Six of them at least died boys. Some grew up, perhaps, never to think of her again, or to think of her year after year with regret for things which might have been. For all of them equally, she was performing a sacrament of remembrance. She was doing exactly what I do when I write a poem. That her poem was of the heart and spirit and mine so much of the mind I put wholly on her side of the tally sheet.

I knew two of Mother's childhood friends well, Marjorie and Rose, both maiden ladies abiding on the street, Hampton Road, where they all had lived as girls. For a time, the three made an effort to stay together. They took up hobbies they might share one night a week at each other's houses, embroidery or Turkish toweling, for instance, that were fine to look at but couldn't be used unless the preacher were coming to dinner.

Mother admonished me not to make fun of Rose. I never saw a reason to. Her vaguely crooked mouth and steady silence seemed dignified to me. It was years before my growing intellect passed her stalled one, and I recognized that Rose was retarded.

In Rose's front yard lay a bed of hybrid iris, neglected since her father's death and slowly vanishing in a thicket of weeds, the gold and purple iris heads still fighting through. In the foyer of the house, someone had built a fountain out of brown and pink tile. Water spurted from a smiling brass dolphin. If one called for her, she stood behind the lattice door long enough for one to contemplate the splashing water. Only when she was sure you'd seen your fill would her thin shadow move behind the marbled glass and that crooked smile appear, ready to be escorted.

Marjorie wore deep green silk and was the sort of person who corrected your grammar. No, that's not quite accurate. She was the sort of person whose rectitude so radiated that one corrected one's own grammar, stuttering so anxiously after perfection that, at last, one preferred to say nothing at all. Some sense that children have for such things told me that Marjorie loved Mother more than Mother loved Marjorie. I thought this gave Mother power, gave her something to parry the extended, expensive education which Marjorie wore without modesty.

Mother retained her past naturally, remaining in contact with it while moving forward. Living your whole life in the city where you were born helps with a sense of permanence and perspective. Periodically I return to Akron to gather fragments of myself, and of her. I remember things by standing where I stood when she told them to me. I'm brought up short by a street name she mentioned, or a house where she once attended a party, or the glare of the windows of the hospital where I was born. I have her high school graduation picture with the names written carefully on the back. Someday I'll dial a phone, knock on a door—

She'd have talked more about her past had she thought of it as completed, as something filed away and requiring particular effort to retrieve. She did not seem to cherish her history because it had not occurred to her that it could be lost. Then she was dead, and I had asked her almost nothing. So I followed her tracks, asking, trying to pick up the pieces, gratified each time somebody answered, "Your mother? Marion Summers? Of course I knew her. Everyone did." I go to my high school reunion or drop into one of my old haunts where it seems pretty likely I'll run into somebody I used to know. The talk may lead around to our parents, and again and again I'm told of some kindness my mother did my friends that she never spoke of, that I had not suspected in the least. I imagine one of those frightened boys shipped off with her address in their uniform pocket, fifty years later, in an unguarded moment confiding to a daughter, a son, a granddaughter, "Yes, your mother was a fine woman, but just between us, there was a girl in Akron, Marion, I never did quite get over."

For several years, I had a recurring dream. As is the case with such things, when I realized what it meant, it retreated and left me to get on with life. The setting is a small modern office building, two floors divided into several suites, quite isolated, standing at the end of a long, lonely road, outside a city whose glow can be seen in the distance. A great bridge stands nearby, though no traffic ever seems to pass over it. In the dream, it is night. I think I am some sort of janitor, because I have the key to some of the suites, but not to all of them. Each occurrence of the dream finds me with keys to different suites, but never to all of them at once. Sometimes there are other people in the building, but inevitably in the suites to which I have no access. Pounding on the windows does not attract their attention. I am alone. This is not necessarily a regrettable situation. My sense is that I have gone to the building, have taken the night janitor job, to isolate myself, to lick psychic wounds which are not mentioned in the dream, but which cause a dull, steady ache in my heart. This particular time, I sense a crisis in the dream. I am determined to throw part of my old self away, the part that is causing the ache, I think. In my hand is my mother's Eastern Star ring, the yellow diamond she wore on special occasions. I slide the ring under the door of one of the locked suites. I stand up and go about my business in the deserted building. Suddenly I want my mother's ring back with an acuteness of longing I have never felt before. I'm bent double with it. I feel I can moan with the pain, because there's nobody there to hear me. I run to the locked door and find that the space between it and the floor has changed so that I can slide my hand under it and grasp the ring on the other side. I seize it and drag it back under the door. The ring is now wrapped in tissue paper. Someone has left it wrapped as a gift. Someone raised the door so I could get my hand under and retrieve it. I sit in the office of the dream cradling the ring in my hand, dumb with gratitude. There is a note tied to the ring, a note in cuneiform, and, of course, I can't read it. But in the dream I know what it says. This knowledge, the message on the ring, is the thing lost at waking.

7. LACE CURTAINS
AND A PORTABLE
EDUCATION

I confuse my name with the name of God in seven languages.
This is a commentary, believe me, not of arrogance,
but of horror.
The bedside poplars, whose cold palms quake by moonlight,
like emperors picked off one by one, answer,
Child, you are taking this too hard.

WHEN, OUT OF IDLE CURIOSITY, I took a look at my employment file at the university where I work, I found a strange entry. Back in the midst of the faculty search that brought me here, my future colleagues agreed mostly to like me, but there was a comment by one, now a good friend, which distressed me. He claimed that in the various interviews and personal conversations I seemed "opaque." Since they hired me, I must not have been *that* opaque, but the comment stuck in my craw. I suspected it was true, though, having nothing to hide, I couldn't understand exactly *why* it was true.

I began addressing the problem of opacity as though it were a question of presentation, of making affect jibe with inner reality. In the midst of that, I realized something more upsetting still. I *was* opaque, not incidentally but essentially, not by accident but by long practice. And I remembered why.

Shown a picture of Mrs. Kramer's 1956 kindergarten class at Betty Jane School on Darrow Road in east Akron, I can name all but two or three of my classmates, all except those who moved away or were in accidents and disappeared. I can tell you one or two of their peculiarities. I can tell you within a season when their birthdays were. That was forty years ago.

The pincerlike retentiveness of my memory would have been merely morbid had I not become a poet, or a spy.

Our class was in the Portable that year. After World War II, the neighborhoods around the school expanded fast, with people moving out of central Akron into the eastern suburbs, with kids being born close upon each other to make up for lost time and, I suppose, to even out the slaughter. There wasn't money to build new schools fast enough, so the city borrowed portable barracks from the army. These green-gray buildings had two huge rooms, one you used for class and one that was a sort of giant entrance hall, unheated, undecorated, drafty, and unlit, where you took off your boots and where you had to sit if you misbehaved. Our class spent two years in the Portable. This was a distinction, whether laudatory or derogatory we never were told. But it made us feel like pioneers.

It was in the Portable that Debbie Marsh showed me how to play house. This was a girl's game, unknown to me before that hour. It was the first time I realized that girls—that other people in general—had as highly evolved and dramatic mythologies as we commando boys did with our ancient warfare in Crines's woods.

In the Portable also, Carolyn Cross kicked a window open onto the world by coloring her Christmas Santa yellow instead of red. This act amazed me. Her Santa was yellow, and no thunderbolt had fallen. Mrs. Kramer completed our lesson in the freedom of the mind by saying "Why not a yellow Santa?" and thumbtacking Carolyn's picture in what we recognized as the place of honor.

We did not object to the Portable as much as our parents did. It was, alternately, too hot and too cold, but it was spacious. It reminded us of the war movies those of us who were boys loved, and it set us apart from the rest of the school. *We are the Portable.* We were recognizable, a cadre. We were assumed to be bad (the other kids had all sorts of stories for why we were there and not they), and we intended to live up to the reputation.

Someone else has already seized the line, "Everything I know I learned in kindergarten," and anyway it is not true in my case, but what I did learn was astonishing then and durable now, and almost always right. Homeschooling disturbs me because, if my recollections are correct, I remember almost nothing that Mrs. Kramer said. Everything came from my playmates-turned-classmates. Among ourselves, we were inventing the language of our generation.

I am thinking of the particular day in the Portable when Mrs. Kramer was absent, and the frazzled substitute gave us mimeographed crossword puzzles to do. They were a little beyond our age, but the poor soul must have been desperate. I already knew about crossword puzzles. My grandmother was a great doer of them. She sat with them in her living room on Hampton Road, in the shadow of the smokestacks of Goodyear Tire. Light filtered onto her carpets through leaves and layers of lace curtains. I watched her thinking hard and then writing with a fat black fountain pen. She used ink that came in jars, and there were always stains on the antimacassars and carpet around the place where she did her puzzles. She worked silently and with such introspective intensity that even now, when somebody asks somebody else one of the clues—"What's a four-letter word for

New Zealander?"—I think a trespass is being committed. Grandmother's silence over the puzzles, her advanced age, and strange wayward Irishness made me think of the puzzles as spells you had to be a witch to do, and in complete silence.

Let me pause for a moment to discourse on Grandmother's lace curtains. The phrase "lace-curtain Irish" has particular meaning to me. My grandparents and their neighbors in Goodyear Heights were not rich by any means—being for the most part laborers in the rubber plants—but they saw no reason why the Hampton Road should know it. There were always lace curtains. At Grandmother's, when they became too tattered for the windows, they went into the drawers of the great black sideboard to have a second life as tablecloths, and, after that, as playthings for the grandchildren. At the time of which I speak, there were only three grandchildren, one of them an infant and the other two boys.

Having discovered the cast-off lace curtains, and with my gender identification still somewhat fluid, I wrapped them around myself, waltzing through Grandmother's rooms as queenly as I knew how, playing bride, playing a painting I had seen where immigrants leave for America, the woman's sadly gay scarf streaming in the wind behind her, playing heroines you encounter in the movies your mother takes you to, with long trailing gowns and lots of swordplay happening around them. I try to remember what fascinated me about those ladies, and for the most part I can't. I think it was simply the clothing, far more demonstrative than male garb as it was in the 1950s, voluminous, alive, able more fully to express the personality of the wearer and the significance of the occasion.

This sort of play distressed my mother for reasons not then clear to me. She asked her mother to hide the lace curtains, which she did. When I found them again, Grandma made a great show of ignoring me so, if I were discovered, she could plead inattention. Grandma's tolerance allowed me to get through the brief transvestite phase of my life—indeed the only period at all when I was particularly interested in personal fashion—without a scar.

Personal lace was a dead issue by the time crossword puzzles became ascendent. Having watched Grandma work the puzzles made me think I knew something about them. That afternoon in the Portable when I took my mimeo sheet, I regarded it for a moment with astonishment. I'd never really *seen* a crossword except backwards through newspaper lit by Grandma's living room windows. Frontways, it was a box of many empty squares and some dark ones. Had there been anything printed on the side, I might have guessed what we were supposed to do.

As it was, I reasoned that there were two things which Grandmother could have been doing with her blue-blue-black ink. Maybe you were supposed to fill in all the little squares, with the already filled-in ones as an example. Maybe you were supposed to put designs in the blank squares, and the filled-in ones were to separate the patterns from each other so they looked more distinctive.

Accordingly I began to draw flowers and *X*s and suns in the white spaces. Carolyn Cross watched me doing it, and, when I was well along, she raised her hand and told the substitute that I had spoiled my paper. I was given another and told to wait for instructions.

It's hard to imagine a more inconsequential moment than this, yet in my mind it remains absolutely indelible. Not for an instant had it occurred to me that there was a *particular* way that people were expected to work a crossword puzzle. I assumed Grandma had just been filling in the spaces as she pleased, in an act of unbridled creativity. I would have guessed she was casting spells, struggling in her own way for images to fit into tiny printed spaces. That there were *rules* for this game shocked me; I had been excluded from a necessary, surprising, and somewhat dismaying truth.

The substitute passed out the second page, where they told you the words that were supposed to go into the spaces, and we started again.

The world changed that day. I saw for the first time that I was not creating everything new. Not only didn't I *have* to, but I wasn't going to be *allowed* to. Before that hour, I'd supposed I was making everything up from scratch. When I'd been corrected for doing something "wrong," I interpreted the occasion as one in which I had tried other people's patience or crossed their desires in some way. That they could make me hurt for it was an aspect of superior size, not superior knowledge. They could correct me because they were bigger, and, when they went away, I would be free again to do it as I pleased.

The crossword, though, was a revelation. There was a right way and everybody seemed to know it but me. I had not merely been overpowered; I had been *wrong*.

The next year, we moved on to the first grade. We were not only in the main building then, but in the new part of the main building, with long windows opening on the playground and on the forested hills of Goodyear Heights Metropolitan Park beyond. This was the "nice surprise" our parents were promised for our having endured the Portable, and, whatever they actually thought, we found it grand recompense indeed. We were still special, for, if we had left the Portable, we were among the first to use the New Building, and to be at the very end of it, where we could get out first when the bell rang.

Universal practice then was to divide a class into reading groups based on the levels of skill. We were to name ourselves after birds; within that parameter, each group got to choose its own name, but I forget this fact when I consider the archetypal resonance of the names we chose. The very brightest and fastest learners were the Bluebirds. The medium readers were the Robins, plain, common, yeomanly. The slow students were the Parrots, chosen with regard to gorgeousness of color and innocent of further connotations. I was a Parrot. I was not getting it. I remember the blank misery of not being able to make an "8," the horror of looking at a page of swimming black marks and being expected to read. Mrs. Rock did not take long to diagnose that I was merely farsighted and unable to see the print in front of my face. I was subjected to the childhood trauma of Coke-bottle glasses-wearing, but spared the worse one of being in the slow class. From then on it was Bluebirds all the way. Yes, I am still proud of it. Yes, there is still a frisson of terror at what might have been had I stayed a Parrot all my life.

Once I was a Bluebird, I went like a house afire.

It was February, and some of us were assigned to do reports on Washington and some on Lincoln. I was in the Lincoln group, and, when it was time for the report, Mrs. Rock stood us in a line so we could make our reports one by one. It filled me with a sense of superiority that all the kids except me had pieces of paper to read from. I felt contemptuous of them, that they couldn't tell a good story without artificial aid.

I was first of the Lincolners to be called upon, and, believe me, I told a good story, about how rich Lincoln had been as a boy, how happy his life was, triumph mounting upon fairy-tale triumph. The beauty of his lady love, wrapped as she no doubt had been in dusty lace. The gallantry of his life in the wilderness. The television show *The Millionaire* was running then, and I recounted Lincoln's adventures creeping about handing million dollar bills to the unsuspecting needy.

To her credit, Mrs. Rock said nothing. I realized I had been, as usual, unique. At first, I expected Mrs. Rock to scold my classmates for cheating off each other, their reports coming with dreary sameness. Identical details, sometimes identical turns of phrase. Surely mine was the best story, and told, I thought, with both spontaneity and wit. But as we went down the line and my classmates read their accounts of the life of Abraham Lincoln, all nearly identical and as wildly opposed to mine as possible—the poverty, the struggle, the tragic death—I began to feel the same sickening sensation as attended the crossword revelation. They knew something I didn't. They knew when Mrs. Rock said the word "report" that they were meant to go and look information up and deliver it exactly as written in the source.

My distress was many-headed. How did they know about *reports?* Who had come to their houses and told them while leaving me in the dark? Who made the rule that a "report" was different from a revery? Why wasn't I told? I was absolutely certain that mine was the better story, livelier and far happier. I was sure Lincoln would have been gladder to have lived the life I gave him. That it should be *wrong* appeared strictly statistical—they all had one story, I another; I was merely outnumbered. This was a defense; eventually I allowed myself to admit I simply had *not known.*

Though I learned lessons from these events, they might not have been fully the ones I should have learned. I should have learned caution and correct procedure. What I did learn was that there would be stunning differences between what different people perceive, and that sometimes, as in the case of the Lincoln report, it would involve a real disparity between truth and fantasy, but at other times, as in the case of the lace curtains, what was going on would seem one thing to the onlooker and another to the participant, and that mutual horror of the other's perspective would leave communication all but impossible. I was not interested in turning into a woman then or thereafter, whatever my mother thought. Parading around in an old lace curtain would not win for me the passive if unanswerable power of a movie star, whatever I thought.

I became good at guessing when this disparity would likely be in effect, and how to fake unanimity and thereby avoid the consequences of nonconformity. My life would have been easier if I had, from the first, put a real value on this choice, as opposed to thinking of it as a matter merely of convenience. Prudence would have taught me to root out my own perceptions when they were at odds with the world's, demonizing them so that my thoughts and the majority's were in actual accord. I did not do this. I kept a double vision that would make me receptive to the ambiguous signals which inform the artist and the mystic, as well as the outcast.

A severer consequence, though, was that, in the years of my boyhood, I was, not frequently but more often than I deserved, accused of being a liar. I always denied the charge, never consciously by adding another lie to the one I was originally accused of. Originally, with my fluid concept of reality, I had no idea what a lie was. When people said I had told one, the simple tone of the accusation sounded so horrible that, of course, I denied it. Plato notwithstanding, even a poet does not lie on purpose; he just has a more inclusive definition of the truth. At one point, I identified "lie" with "insult," assuming I had hurt people's feelings in some obscure way. Sometimes I recognized that the thing I described might not actually have happened, but the distinction between "should have happened" and "really happened" was immaterial. It had not occurred to me that the activity of invention was perceived to be different from the activity of discovery.

For a period, I would fantasize about having an adopted brother. *Adopted* was the important part, for it would signify he was not really from the dull round of things which made our family what it was and with which I was already deeply bored. When I told the wife of our Evangelical and Reformed preacher that we were getting a brother, it was to share the crowning detail of months of revery, worked out in exquisite detail, even as to where my brother would sleep, what games we would play, where we would explore. When I said it, I meant it as witness of an alternate and preferable reality. Didn't grownups make things up all the time? Weren't there movies and books and jokes, all presenting imaginary situations meant, for the moment at least, to be taken as truth?

When word came back to my mother, she said, angrily, "Now Mrs. Deppen knows you are a liar." I couldn't defend myself, for I understood that what I said was not in fact true in the sense my mother required. I felt betrayed by Mrs. Deppen. I'd told a fairy story, to have it corrected as though it were an arithmetic exam.

Such moments led periodically to terrible crossroads, at each one of which I was invited to decline the world of my internal birthright—vivid and anarchic—in favor of generally agreed-upon reality. Life would have been easier if I had done so, maybe, or perhaps it would have led to the psychosis which springs from truly elemental denial. The world exhibited some grace in that I was able to weather the consequences of keeping a whole spirit. I rejected neither option, neither the internal nor the external, becoming neither wholly successful nor utterly maladroit at what people call "life." I did not give up the visions that enlarged and delighted my childhood, but I learned when to speak of them and when not. Mostly not, as it turns out.

Except on paper. Except in poetry.

That is part of the blessing of writing, and why it is better than conversation. One can relate anything one wishes, without enduring directly the expressions on the reader's face. The oddest question people ask me about things I've written is, "Now, did that *really* happen?" Even when I know whether it "happened" or not, I never know what to say. The answer is always yes, but in what sense might take a bit of explanation.

When I went to college up in Portage County, at Hiram, one of the important things that happened to me in the important freshman year was someone's handing me a copy of J. R. R. Tolkien's *The Hobbit*. By the time I finished burrowing through the entire Tolkien *corpus* as it stood then—missing classes, shunning meals, reading until my eyes slammed shut with exhaustion—I realized I had found not only the great imaginative achievement of the twentieth century (I still hold this opinion, though it dare not be breathed on a Modernism-saturated college campus) but also the mind who so nearly embodied my own world view that I think I might have been ruined as a writer if I had encountered him even a few months earlier. I would happily have spent my imagination's time annotating Middle Earth, wandering in a country revealed rather than invented, and though that is death for a poet, I would not have regretted it that much, as it was so much like *home*. But I had tasted Blake and Yeats, had written a little of my own, had stepped a few steps down a path a little less high and remote than Middle Earth, but my own. Though I'd wander the beautiful roads of Hiram on a spring day revolving Tolkien's story in my head as though it were my own, I did manage to break free. I read *Lord of the Rings* once every few years, a visitor rather than a citizen. On each reading, I am struck by the perfection of the vision, everything in its place plausible, inevitable. I still long to own the power of the vision if not the vision itself. I resent that such lightning cannot strike twice in an age.

Even before I began my wanderings in Middle Earth, I realized that I was, as I understand the word, a mystic, and this was yet another thing that could not be whispered to anyone.

I knew things which were in my circumstances and by ordinary means unknowable. Part of my command of anomalous and obscure facts was due to my being a bookworm, but part of it was due to receptivity to voices which spoke to me in my room

and on the paths of the city parks where I lumbered my cautious—and therefore attentive—way. I do not claim this as a
virtue or a distinction, but as an accident. Part of the amazement
of youth was discovering that these perceptions did not come to
everybody, that not everyone could look at a flower and know its
name without, so far as I remembered, having seen it before. I
am still not sure that people are not lying about this. Perhaps all
do, in fact, live portions of their life in Faerie, of which they do
not tell, which makes my failing not weirdness but rather lack of
discretion. I blabbed everything at the first and only later learnt
to keep the mystery. Were people more offended that I lived in a
world they could not enter, or that I had given away a secret? I
always suspected the latter.

My inner life was of a vividness and complexity which, at
selected times, circumvented the exterior world. Going to bed
was not the trauma for me it was for many children. For them,
being put to bed was to be excluded from life. For me, it was to
begin it. I would lie in the dark and think. Thinking was palpable and sensuous. I longed for uninterrupted time to do it, to be
flapping the organs of thought as a fledgling beats its wings in
the nest. The toys and animals on my shelves helped me. I would
beam my thoughts around the room and ask what we should
imagine before sleep, each toy having its turn on a different
night. Tonight my stuffed dog Pluto, tomorrow the imp-shaped
homemade kite hanging on the wall, then the wax Sleeping
Beauty I had gotten out of a cereal box, then the bank shaped
like a moon into which coins could be hurled by a tiny rocket on
a spring. We were a corporate intelligence. When I imagined
things, the pictures played in their consciousness, too. I gave life
to the objects which had put themselves into my world. With a
shock, as I write these words, I realize that my life, which has appeared solitary in many respects, has been peopled with ani-
mated multitudes. I have felt alone only when I stepped out of

My vision into Ours, the world's, and felt the Presences vanish.

Such operations were secret. By that time, I'd learned to put distance between inner life and outer life—not that one was more real to me, but that it was so to everybody else, and to speak of your own world too often or too vividly was to invite scorn. The command, "It's time to start living in the real world, boy," did not encourage me to do so, but rather struck me as an admonition born at once of tyranny and ignorance. It advised only, "keep your mouth shut." I did. It advised, "keep your heart open and secret." I did.

I was a secretive child. I was happiest behind a closed door. I am an opaque adult. My employment folder says so. I know how to make this appear to be what I really want. Secrecy is a strategy almost impossible to unlearn. The only option is to make the two worlds one from the other direction, which is to say, to make the inner world plausible and beautiful to the mass of men. This is the power of the artist, and the only power I ever really wanted.

Let me add that not to have wanted other things was an error. The artist's peace is fully in the process of getting, never in the satisfaction of having, and to be part of the process one sacrifices the rest of one's life, including the things one might actually have *had*. This is not to lodge a complaint, but to record an ambiguous wonder. Would I rather have been the quarterback than the class poet? Yes, oh, yes. But denied one role, one clutches the other like a treasure, one which turns out, providentially, to remain after quarterbackery runs to fat and bad joints.

❊

We must get over shame in the face of our desires. The truth is, finally, that one possesses permanently nothing but need. We expect to be chained to need. We are used to it. Do not recognize ourselves without it. When need is filled, suddenly to the brim and over, there are few adequate responses. Of the lepers Christ healed, only one came back to thank him. The rest, I suspect, were not so much ungrateful as dumbfounded. Were I to wake tomorrow morning and discover I am the man I have desired to be, I do not know how I could take the first step. Except to sing of it, except to begin a poem which to finish were to create a further unfulfilled desire.

If grief is the mother of poetry, joy is the mother of a blessed silence.

8. THE DESCANT GIRLS

This poem is for the great ladies, the goddesses
who preside over the heart of man, which is
my heart, over my heart which is the heart of men.

Tell the world to trash its heap of words.
I have the syllable to start.

AMONG FLUORESCENT INSECTS is a group, normally caterpillars, that glows because they have been infected by a glowing bacterium. What appears to be—and is, from an observer's perspective—rare beauty, is fatal to its bearers. They are dying of a luminous disease.

That is poetry.

The fact is that skill will not avail without passion, and even passion will not avail without incident. The man prays for peace, justice, harmonious love; the poet prays for a life-defining incident. The Poetry Doctor travels about with his syringe, not curing, but giving the disease.

I'm walking down the street with a friend, who grabs my elbow and stops me. "Are you going to do the whole cantata or what?" It takes me a minute to comprehend what he means: I've been singing, softly but relentlessly. Rather than being fully there, on the street, at the present time, with him, I have been in my own world, accompanied by a tune which, unless you're the one making it, must seem a little strange. I shut up, but I remember the tune, so to go over it when I get home, so to understand why it returns to me with such clarity, what might it want from me after all these years.

The song came from church camp. It is called "The Ash Grove." I was happy to have it running in my brain again; I had missed it. But I knew it hadn't come to please me. It had come to please itself, as all the subjects of poetry do.

The verses are about this old soul who wanders around in a grove of trees remembering his departed friends. He sees their faces in the leaves, hears their voices in the whispering of the breeze. At camp, whenever it was our tent's turn to select a song after dinner, I'd shout "The Ash Grove" fast, before another selection could be made. Most everybody liked "The Ash Grove," so I got away with it.

"The Ash Grove" has a nice lilting Welsh tune, but what killed me was when certain of the girls, high schoolers and select eighth graders, came in with music that wasn't written down, a sweet descant, pure, clear, and ravishing. You looked at them when they were singing to see how they did it so high and clear, but to a girl they'd have this featureless serenity on their faces, like people asleep or blissfully deceased. Who wouldn't love them, singing like that, bliss burning across their faces with the morning light?

At church camp, there were clear divisions among kids, informal but ironclad. Boys were the Athletes, the Preachers-to-be, the Studs, the Hippies, the Others. Usually one Brain and one Queer, often the same person. The classifications are pretty self-explanatory. I was, except for one notable occasion, an Other, which suited me for the most part, because of its greater fluidity. I didn't understand the hierarchy of the girls as well, but as far as I could tell there were the Populars, the Preachers'-wives-to-be, the Old Maids, the Hippies, and the Ash Grove Descant Girls. There were no visible girl brains or queers at summer camp. Again, most of these you recognize. But the Ash Grove descant girls were puzzlers. Nobody chose them; they recognized each other, and the first time you sang "The Ash Grove" a given summer, you'd hear the descant rising by some mystical agreement from various places at once, the voices moving together, individuals melting into a heavenly choir, never again for the duration of the summer to part company.

I couldn't figure out the Ash Grove descant principle of selection but guessed it had something to do with spiritual state, for, though the descant girls were often the best singers, it wasn't necessarily so. If you were the daughter of a preacher, even a rebellious daughter, it was a birthright. Dawn, our problematic preacher's kid, did a creditable Ash Grove descant without being able to sing, so far as I could tell, very remarkably in any other song. There was always one Venus from the popular girls—a Judith, a Susanna—the signal that the state of the spirit could not be read accurately by the flesh. The balance of descant singers were drawn from the Old Maid subdivisions of Skags or Fat Girls or the Otherwise Indistinguishable, as a sort of compensation, I guess, for the foreseeable misery of their lives.

I sometimes think that if I could have figured out the Ash Grove descant system I could have had life under better control, not that it was so important by itself, but it was like the first step of a long stair of social comprehension, and if you tripped *there* you're bound to keep on tripping. Related, but perhaps more important, is the notion that I could have understood the unfairness of genius, which taps those who do not love it, ignores those who would give their lives for it. The Ash Grove descant girls did nothing visible to deserve the honor; it just came; they opened their mouths, and it was there.

The descant was only a few bars, and the girls didn't sing it all the time, communicating the proper moment by sonar audible only to themselves. But hearing it as often as possible used to be for me a personal goal. Not in my wildest dreams did I imagine myself singing it. The goal was simply to remember it, so that if everyone else who had gone to summer camp suddenly vanished from the earth there would still be someone who knew and could corner some girl somewhere and provoke her into singing it. That it was singable by *someone* was the world's gift to me.

I *could* have sung "The Ash Grove" descant. It wasn't *forbidden*. But it never seemed right. First, there was the gender issue. Never did men or boys sing it. No, that's not true, but the ones who did were queer, or boy sopranos from that really High church near Cleveland, which amounted to the same thing. Singing was not essentially a male activity at camp; we did it, but we were not supposed to like it or to be especially good at it. I didn't and I wasn't, so in that at least I was straight on the line.

Beyond that was the conviction that the descant music didn't belong to me, that I wasn't entitled to sing it even if I were alone and nobody cared who I was. The moment of the descant was sacred to the initiates, though it seemed like just another camp song to the laity. You had to be chosen. I could let loose with "I Sing a Song of the Saints of God" or "Jacob's Ladder" or "John Jacob Jingleheimer Schmidt" but not "The Ash Grove."

I've got a picture graven in my mind of the descant girls singing with arms around each others' waists, in perfect purity and unselfconsciousness. Even we boys, the studs and the troublemakers and the felons-to-be, settled down for a moment and listened.

As I said, in the verses the person sees the faces of his lost ones in the pattern of lights and shadows in the leaves. This kid Paul who went to camp with us claimed it was because the Welsh hung their dead up in ash branches to rot away, and that the faces were literally there, in assorted stages of decomposition. Paul was older, and I believed him. Oddly, even that didn't harm the story but rather added to its poignancy; plus, I gained respect for the guts necessary to go to such a foul place and look on the horror that was all that remained of someone you loved. That was the definition of heroic to me. That was the courage that it took to *discover,* to write something more vital than a sonnet lamenting your student loans.

That night, the night after my friend asks me why I'm singing that song so much, I go to the crafts store at the mall and buy paints and those stupid plaster casts of fruit and smiling pirates and the Last Supper. I don't know why, but it is *necessary.* I buy the plaster figurines and scurry for the exit. Home, I spread newspapers on the table, lay out my stuff, and begin to paint. I don't know why. It's brute action, demanded by the muscles. My hand revels in the big brush sweeps of the backgrounds, in the small gestures of the brush putting the right colors (or wrong colors) in the creases of the tiny eyes and fingers of the plaster figures. My hand remembers something. I keep painting. I'm wondering all the while, why am I doing this? My body knows something I don't. It wants me to remember something I am not ready to remember. It makes me paint these stupid crafts I'll have to throw away when I'm done. I'm doing such an awful job, wanting to do well but knowing it doesn't matter, that only the participation counts. Haven't felt like this since summer camp.

Summer camp.

A face.

A door swung wide for the first time.

A *story.*

9. THE SERPENT
AND THE GROVE

Ferret comes to nibble from my hand.
Thrush takes its small food.
In dreams I am sustained by compassionate wild eyes.
In dreams the animals aid me
for my animal
as God shall never aid me for my god.

THERE WAS A PHOTO of me hoisting a bedroll onto the tailgate of my father's car. My hair lies close, in the Marine butch cut popular with boys my age. I am eleven. My sister is five and, to an impartial observer, the focus of the picture, with her curly-haired energy, the ruffle of her homemade plaid dress in the breeze, the uncomplicated smile as she watches me struggle with the bedroll, which, consuming the foreground, seems larger than either of us. Though the photo is in black and white, anyone who remembers the scene colors it with our red hair, with the vivid blue plaid of my sister's dress, the fuzzy robin's-egg of the blanket. The summer sky, too, is blue, but incomparably subtler and more solemn. My white shirt bears an unobtrusive geometric pattern, a design favored as vacation wear by the men of our family for flamboyance still asserting a basic conservatism. I don't especially like the shirt, but mother packed eight shirts for eight days, this being the last day and the last shirt. One does not know for certain the identity of the photographer, though from the slight retreat in my posture, the ineffectual crook of the elbow—as though already resigned to failure in the effort to lift the bedroll—one assumes it is Father.

The expression on my sunburned face is at once unremarkable and complicated. For the first time, I worry about the way I look. I'm a plain child covering up my plainness by making it seem intentional. I'm making a face at the camera. The lens surprises me midway in a struggle so intimate that the invasion is at once unforgivable and unacknowledgable, the violation of privacy not yet granted by the world.

The next instant would reveal whether I laugh or cry, but the camera turns away.

I remember it like yesterday. The highway runs flat in the Ohio light. The air sags with the pungency of road kills. Deep in the country, we turn onto a one-lane road snaking between thickets of wild rose. The fields lie silver from dust and roses. Cows gnaw through dust to the grass underneath, their mouths and pelts coated like fairies in a pageant with the glitter of silica blown from the eroding hills. I feel a vague sense that the panorama is spread out to teach me something.

At the road's end, a sign reads, "Templed Hills Christian Campground." Under the letters are painted a crown and a world surmounted by an elongated cross, as though it were a rocket aiming a trail of vapor at the little painted world beneath it. Father turns on the spray to clean the windshield, creating a green soup of dust and smashed bugs. Through the brightening glass loom two hills and barnlike structures perched at different levels on them.

"Are those the temples?"

"What temples?"

"You know. Templed Hills. Are those the temples?"

Mother says, "It's just a name."

The answer does not satisfy. I peer steadily, looking for the temples which must be hidden among the trees. I want to go home but cannot say so. The expectant silence of the ride has set up a decorum that I'd shatter by seeming to be unhappy. The singing birds are the same as home.

I get out of the car, stand at the tailgate waiting for Father to unlock the bedroll and suitcase. My sister comes close. The nearest building is so obviously a dining hall that she points to more distant ones and says,

"Are those the temples?"

I say, "It's just the name." I catch her peering, as I did, through the trees for something more.

"What am I supposed to do now?"

"Wait. Someone will come. Someone must have seen the dust."

Mother coughs when father says, "dust."

A man emerges from the forest in a white T-shirt and cutoffs. Around his neck he wears a rough oval of wood on a plastic cord. He smiles, his big teeth like the teeth of men in magazines, straight and milk colored. I recognize him as a young man, much younger than my father. He extends his hand and says,

"I'm Mark. I'm your counselor. I praise God that you could come."

I know I must reach for his hand, but I stand back from my own hand as far as possible, putting distance between us. Mark says something to my parents. My sister asks a question and Mark answers, patiently, thoroughly, like someone not used to children.

Mark leads me to a table in the maple shade. The leaves of the maples are mined and torn by insects; light comes through in scribbles. On the table lie woodburning instruments connected to the dining hall by black extension cords. Mark selects a piece of wood, the cross section of a branch. A cherry branch, the purple smooth bark and the eyelike lenticels.

Mark says, "I want you to burn your name in this so we all know who you are. Just like I have. Decorate it up nice with these."

Elderberries and dandelion heads and bits of bloodroot peek from cardboard boxes. I burn my name into the wood, settling for Dave, as I normally would not, to avoid bending forever over the woodburners while my family waits, this time very patiently. I expect Father to call, to tell me I'm taking too much time, but the only sounds are red-winged blackbirds, wind, tires over dusty gravel, sometimes Mark saying how beautifully I burn the wood. I smear the wood purple with elderberry. Without being told, I poke plastic lanyard cord through drilled holes and tie it around my neck.

I say "finished" and walk back to the car, wondering if that's what I came to learn. Where the car was is a space of blue light.

"Where are they? Where's my mother?"

Mark smiles. He says, "We do this on purpose. It's easier for first-time campers. Saying goodbye can be awfully hard . . ."—he lifts the nameplate from the my chest—. . . "Davy."

Nobody calls me Davy. I concentrate on that, trying to believe it's what's making me feel bad. There's something heavy in my stomach. There has been a violation somewhere, though by Mark or my parents I don't know. I burst into tears. This is not usual. Reticence is prized in my family. I struggle to hold them back. They push out. Mark leans over to dry the tears with the edge of his T-shirt, but I pull away.

❀

Seven hundred paces into the forest, unless I lose count, we come to the tent. The tent's high and airy, giving the impression of a great green room, though the green and the room belong to the forest beyond the rolled flaps. I take a bottom bunk, a gesture of politeness, assuming others—the honored longtimers—will want the top. I try to shove my suitcase under the bed, so nobody will see my eight shirts and four pairs of shorts, folded by mother as though they were back home in a dresser drawer. But the mattress sags down to the floor. I drag the suitcase out again and arrange it in the space at the end of the bed, hoping to remember to open it only while it is dark.

Mark says, "Feeling better?"

I say, "Yes."

Boys appear at the door, one by one. These will be my associates, perhaps adversaries, for the next week. Ryan is a boy soprano. He likes to sing songs from World War I. He is a relief; now none of the rest of us males will have to sing very much. Like a peacock in a barnyard, he will make us all invisible.

Paul comes, the Big Kid. He wants a top bunk. I hope he'll take the bunk over mine, but Paul says, "What are you staring at, faggot?" and takes the bunk nearest Mark.

Then Avi, who is from Israel and wears letters that look like golden fire on a chain around his neck. Nobody but Avi will be able to say "Jew" all week, even as only Leon, the black guy in the first tent, can start talking about blacks. Leon's in the first tent for the sake of visitors, so they can see right off we have all sorts of people. Avi's words rise on the end, like someone singing. Leon says "man" even to the girls. We say "man," too, but are far more precise in usage.

Allen comes, sweating from the afternoon sun. He's fat, and I wait for Paul to call him a name. Paul smiles, extends his hand, says, "Hiya, Porky." After that nobody remembers "Allen," only "Porky."

Ricky comes next, crying, his mother with him, though Mark tries to keep her at the car. It's hard to remember Ricky because he never recovers from his homesickness, and the next morning he's gone, like a dead child bundled away by night.

Terry and Jerry are brothers. Terry goes on to the next tent.

Jerry stays. He takes a magnifying glass out of his pocket to fry ants that crawl across the boards in the sun dappling through the maples.

Mark says, "Would you like the ants to do that to you?"

Jerry moves the glass out of focus and says, "I was just looking."

Last comes Brad, marching through the forest alone with a bright blue pack on his back. Mark says, "I'm sorry, I thought—" but Brad smiles and says, "There's no need for apology," the way one does when there is. He sounds grown up. Normally I would find that irritating.

"I could come after all. Dad cleared it with the director. Said it would do me good. Can I sleep here?" he says, pointing to the vacant bunk over me.

"Sure."

I try to figure Brad out, figure what's between him and Mark that must be apologized for. His hair lies in easy curls, the color of dark honey. I touch my own hair, wishing it to thin and curl like Brad's, wishing to grow two inches so I could see what he sees. Brad smells of sunlight, like someone sitting in a field. He tries out his bunk. I see the contour of his body above him in the canvas. It seems foreign, not a body, but like looking at a contour map of mountains and valleys upside down. I reach out and touch the lowest point.

Paul's watching. Paul says, "Faggot."

I don't know the word, exactly, though Paul's said it three times. I think it means creep or something, but plainly there's more. Mark says, "I don't want to hear that word again." Paul mouths it silently when Mark's back is turned.

We wait for more boys, but that's all that's coming. A bell rings beyond the trees. Mark says, "Supper. Come on, chowhounds."

Before we reach the dining hall, Paul is calling me "brains."

Maybe I mentioned I am a scholarship boy. Maybe it's because I used the word "vocabulary" in a sentence Paul could hear.

I say, "I don't like that."

"Aw," Paul says, "the _____ doesn't like it." He doesn't say "faggot," but leaves a space in the sound while he mouths the syllables. I figure "brains" is better than "faggot," whatever it means.

Paul begins to sing: "Six little ducks that I once knew, fat one, skinny one, Porky too...," grinning toward Allen with a face that is already handsome. Mark starts to laugh, but he sees Porky's misery and says, "Now—." I feel glad when Paul's interest shifts from me to Porky, then guilty for feeling it.

The dining hall's close, and Paul hasn't time for a second chorus. I sit so I can look at Brad. Tall, but not big like Paul, thin, still a boy. Pale eyes. Green. Like my grandmother's ring, watery jade. I watch Brad while they introduce the counselors from the other tents. They all seem to be named Chuck and Tina. Buck-toothed Tina. Tiny Tina. Fat Chuck. Grizzled Chuck. The campers must stand up and tell what church they're from. I say,

"David Hopes, Emmanuel United Church of Christ, Akron."

Paul says, "Yeah, Brains!" and everybody laughs. Not a bad laugh, either.

❄

After supper, programs and discussion. Brad knows that we always count off by fives, so just before count-off he moves me so there are four campers between us, and we're in the same group.

❄

Back in the tent after the excitement of the day, we talk while Mark organizes the bedding-down. The first night we all tell a story. My story is so horrifying that I become the tent storyteller. I tell tales from Poe, or Saturday afternoon monster movies changed so nobody will recognize them. My own voice in the dark amazes me, the idea that everyone is listening, the clarity that seems to belong to someone else, the words pronounced perfectly, phrases forming in the middle of the air. After the story, Ryan sings. Mark wants him to sing a hymn, which he will do if he is allowed first to sing "Just Before the Battle, Mother" or "Tenting Tonight." They are very sad songs, and they change the emotions in the tent from the excitement of the monster stories into something easier to sleep on. Mark has to say, "OK, simmer down" a couple of times. When quiet comes, I feel Brad's arm descending in the dark, so we can shake hands goodnight.

Raccoons wrestle for crumbs under the floorboards. I think I am the only one who hears them.

Mornings we spend in classes. Because I'm a scholarship boy and meant to do something useful for my church, I've chosen a class in Creative Worship, where we're made bold to read poems or sing songs in front of the altar, to "break with tradition and bring new perspectives." I picture myself home, reading poetry and playing rock and roll records, the old people smiling, trying to like the idea. Brad picked one in Contemporary Problems of Youth, where you read *To Kill a Mockingbird* and *A Separate Peace*. I watch him across the little yard between us. When I look up, he's watching me. He smiles, though I'm usually too embarrassed and just look, as though an interesting bird or the movement of the trees had just then captivated me.

The imperative at meals is to avoid Paul, or at least to avoid Paul and Porky together. Porky can't lift a fork to his mouth without Paul's commenting. Forbidden to wise-mouth by a Chuck or a Tina, he works his handsome boy-man face into a smirk, which has the same effect.

"Hey, Pork, more butter?"

"Porky, my man, how about thirds?"

Nor can Porky win by eating nothing at all. If he fasts, Paul stands during announcements and bellows, "Hey, campers,

Porky's on a diet!" Everybody laughs when Paul laughs. I think it's because he's big and handsome, with a voice almost changed. Porky stares at his plate, trying to calculate the right pace, the right portions to excite the least comment. I try to love Porky as a Christian, but I can't get past fat and misery.

Dawn comes to Porky's aid. It's something she would do. She says to the girls at her table when they giggle at Paul's Porky routine, "I don't think that's very Christian." That makes them giggle all the harder.

I keep silent, knowing Paul waits for a provocation to call me "faggot" or "brains." Nonattachment takes a Christian stronger than I. Dawn seems up to it, though maybe it's more natural to a preacher's kid.

At worship, we sing hymns telling the stories of saints and martyrs, reasonable saints mostly, the kind palatable to Protestants. It's possible to be among them, the hymns say. At the end, we sing "The Ash Grove."

Paul doesn't sing the hymns or the camp songs, but he'll sing "The Ash Grove." I try not to look at him then, in case I start to like him. The girls hit the descant on the last verse. I can sleep beautifully if I hear that before bedtime.

❄

My skin burns, then tans. My hair changes to the color of corn silk. For the first time, I sit in the sun a little longer, try combing my hair in a different way, thinking of what Brad might want to look at.

The camp employees use the pool in the afternoon. Deirdre, the second cook, appears on the edge with her long hair unpinned. Deirdre has breasts, curves, and hair with a sensual existence of its own. Black when wet, it dries in the sun to mahogany. When Deirdre swims, the campers back against the sides of the pool to watch. Each afternoon, she swims twelve laps and pulls herself out with blue swimsuit clinging. She waves goodbye, smiling, having done everything on purpose. The breastless church girls paddle in to take the pool back.

❅

Before breakfast and supper come private times when we're expected to find a log or a stone or the crook of a tree on which to meditate. Grizzled Chuck gathers us from the pool and says we'll try something new. Each is to find a Home in the Woods, a secret place to commune with the God of Nature. At other times, we might laugh out loud at talk like this, but at Templed Hills it sounds right. Paul winds up for a crack, but Mark digs his fingers into his shoulder. It looks like a pat of affection, but Paul's skin dimples under Mark's nails.

Without our planning it exactly, my path and Brad's converge that evening. Nobody said the Spirit couldn't lead two of us to the same Home in the Woods. We join like two rivers at the low point of the path. Sometimes as we walk, Brad puts his hand at the small of my back. Whenever I feel it, I look sharp into the trees, thinking Brad means to call my attention to something.

"Nothing," he says. "Just keeping in touch."

Maple wood. Spruce wood. Bog. Open space. We walk so long we'll have to run to get back when the bell rings dinner. We let the Spirit of Nature lead us at first, but minutes pass, and we begin to look for likely places, deciding that what the Spirit wants is commitment from us. Choosing seems so much less than being led that we hesitate.

Brad says, "Do you feel It?"

"I don't know. You?"

Brad shrugs, also unsure what "it" might feel like.

Brad says, "We could pray."

I can't account for why praying doesn't strike the right note. I look west. The sun shipwrecks in the high tulips. Thrushes commence evening chorus, one by one, beginning with a single bird on the rim of the world.

"Nice."

Brad answers, "Yeah," touching the sunlight on my back.

We both feel before we see. A shiver mistakable for wind parts the rusty grass of the clearing. We watch it for a moment before the sharp intake of breath that means *snake*.

Campers are informed of the blacksnakes that destroy the rats of farmers' barns, how they are good and must never be killed. But this is no mere barn snake. Black, a thread of an unraveled world, it rivers through the clearing from one patch of woods toward another. We follow its approach, huge, lustrous, up close not black at all, but gleaming midnight blue, a color I don't expect on a living thing. In our hearts, in a single moment, we understand that never before has this snake been seen. It is Eden, and this is the Snake before the Fall. It is the first sighting of the Serpent. We can call it anything. It keeps coming. We stand frozen, pictures of people inanimate with fascination and fear. Blood pumps in our ears; no, it is not fear. For the first time, I feel that sensation under my shorts, that achy hardness which one day will be so familiar. I have nothing to account for it then. It frightens me so badly I do not touch it.

The snake reaches Brad first, gliding across his sneakers, cobalt and anthracite over dirty white. Even looped to go among the grasses, it is six feet long. Brad feels the scales of its belly graze his ankle. Shivering, he whispers, "It's warm."

The snake hesitates before my leg. I try not to move. It flicks its tongue, lifts its head from the ground to get a wider taste. The eyes are not radiant like the creature's body, but absorbent, tunnels leading in. Its head rubs against the bare of my calf. It is scratching itself on me. I feel the thrill through my nerves. The snake flutters its tongue against my skin. I hold my breath as long as I can, then breathe in shallow pants. The snake leans back onto the ground, whiplashes forward with untraceable speed, and vanishes. I can't seem to get my breath steadied for a while.

"Not poisonous," Brad says, as if the cobalt spearhead still lay against my leg.

I start to say "shit" as I would back home, but the holiness of the moment stops me. I raise my head. Brad turns to see what I see.

We see the wood the snake came from. Six clean-trunked tulips support a green roof, maples and dogwood and sassafras descending in green planes beneath. The interior of the wood is lit deep by the rays of the sun; setting, it silvers the pillar tulips, transforms the confusion of leaves to liquid gold. The wood thrush, surprised from behind by the sun, trills in plain sight. With one voice we say,

"The Temple!"

It is *not* just a name, as I always knew.

The dinner bell is ringing when we enter the wood. Neither of us hesitates. We throw shadows tall as trees.

❈

Our absence disorganizes the evening's activities. The campers eat dinner overwrought by that mixture of curiosity and horror that comes when there is danger. More confessions, more conversions than usual. Unspoken "what-if's" haunt the conversations. They've seen too many movies, heard too many campfire chillers, expect the worst. Someone goes to take a glance in the pool. Grizzled Chuck and a few of the Tinas stay to supervise while Mark and the others search.

They meet us coming down the wood path, almost home on our own. Fat Chuck is angry, and Mark has to stand in front of him.

Mark says, "Where were you?"

I feel the truth come to my mouth. It hadn't occurred to me that anyone would be angry, or even notice. I start to say, "We went—," before Brad stops me with a touch on the arm.

Brad says, "We got lost. Sorry."

Mark says, "I know about you. I want Davy to answer. I want the truth. Davy?"

I don't answer. My mind concentrates on what Mark has just said.

I know about you.

What? . . . what does he know?

I search my conscience for what there is to be ashamed of, for a reason for the anger on the men's faces. If the choice is between Brad and fact, it's no contest. I say, "We got lost. We're really sorry."

"What did you do?"

"Nothing," Brad says, too fast.

What do you know? What shouldn't we have done?

Into the silence I say, "We saw the snake."

The men lead us back to camp and give us supper. They sit watching us eat, smiling gradually and talking normal, forgiving whatever we'd done. We haven't missed evening presentation, where Dawn and girls from her cabin put on a skit about racial prejudice.

❧

Each meditation period, each free period, finds us on the Temple path. At noon, the little wood is no more interesting than the grown-over farmland surrounding it. But at morning and evening, it becomes the Temple, filled with slanted holy light, radiant and mysterious. It's not necessary even to enter fully. If time is short, one can run the gnat-tormented path through the trees, take it in with a glance at a distance, run back, and hardly be missed. The look suffices. But if there's time to enter and wait, we do, to see the snake, that blue lightning no more stirred by our presence than if we'd been two saplings. It is always there, waiting.

Mark follows once. It's his duty to know what we're up to. We understand. He comes at noon, when under plain sun it's another clump of trees. We're not even sure he's looking in the right place. He says "Nice," and turns away, satisfied, or bored, which in this case is better.

Ryan comes at twilight. He senses his separateness from us and sits a little off away on the log. When the light reaches a certain angle, Ryan, like the thrush, begins to sing. He sings "Tenting Tonight," as he does when no one suggests anything else. In the Temple, we realize how beautiful his voice is, small and fragile under the open sky. We can imagine it's a hundred years ago on a bitter battlefield if we shut our eyes and don't look at his Cleveland Browns T-shirt. We tell Ryan he can come there any time if he wants. I don't know that he ever does. Ryan's not one for adventures in the woods.

That evening at meditation, after Ryan has blessed the place unexpectedly with his song, on our log above the sea of mayapples, Brad sits behind with his arms around me, pulling me tight against his body. It makes us one person. We breathe together. We hear, feel, see together so intimately that we don't have to point and say "Look" when something happens. I cannot remember being so happy, or rather being happy in that way. I had the joy of my thoughts in solitude, which is a great joy, but this was different, the joy of togetherness, which I had never felt before, and never would, with such purity and perfection, again.

Minute follows minute, and still there's no dinner bell, only the pressure of Brad's hands on my belly, his breath on the hair at the back of my neck. I don't know what to say, so I say nothing. I put my hands over his where they press my belly. I think I'm a golden liquid, thick, honey colored, sun colored. I think we are flowing into each other.

On schedule, the Guardian slides to his twilight hunt.

Our legs swing from the log at once, make it to camp in time for the dinner bell.

We arrive before the prayer. We have learned our lesson. Over the empty place settings I hear Paul start up:

On top of old Porky,
All covered with fat . . .

There are probably more verses, but I don't mean to take a chance. I say, calm as I can, as though we were friends, "Paul, shut up."

"What?"

"And stay shut up."

Paul looks at me carefully, expecting a joke. It's no joke. His handsome face reddens.

Like a carnivore drawing blood, I see this and am emboldened by it. I say, "Nobody thinks you're funny."

I want to add, "Least of all _____" but I can't remember Porky's real name. At the next table, Dawn puts her hands together in a pantomime of applause. Amid this company, there's nowhere for Paul to put his fury. He moves to another table, saying out loud, "I can't stand faggots." He's too angry for Mark to shush this time.

Brad and Porky and I talk like friends, passing dishes gallantly to the girls across the table. We realize Porky really is funny, a deadly mimic who has had plenty of occasion to sharpen his Paul. The instant I acknowledge Porky's humor, I remember his name.

"Allen," I say, as though the girls across the table had asked to be introduced.

Brad whispers in my ear, "Proud of you, man." I'm flush and happy; the camp chow mein is honey on our tongues.

Brad's got KP that night, so the half hour between supper and evening program I have to myself. I walk out onto the bent green hill. June bugs zoom against me till I move away from the light. I'm not afraid of the dark, though I people it with monsters as all my friends do. Why? All shapes are the shapes of the Guardian. It begins to make sense. *I shall fear not.*

The Templed Hills all-girls-except-Ryan choir practices before evening program, "Wondrous Love." I hear Ryan, of course, but also Dawn's clear, persistent alto, buttressing the wavering line of her sisters. I like her, a little, her life that's like her voice singing, shoring up the weaknesses of the world, shining out where needed, fading back where others are strong. I say the name "Dawn" out loud to get the feel of it. Maybe I'll like her when we get back home. Everyone at church expects us to have a relationship, and maybe we would if we could stop hating each other. I think I have the dislike stopped first. I say, "Dawn—"

Before "Dawn" dies from my tongue, my head jerks forward, struck behind, almost at exact center. I know without turning around that it's Paul. No one else could hit from that angle or with that strength. I don't want to give him the satisfaction of falling, but my knees bend like water and I taste gravel in my mouth. Then there is nothing.

I couldn't have been unconscious for more than a minute, but long enough for Paul to panic. I wake in his arms, the handsome face contorted high up in the air, his man's voice repeating, "You all right?" in a whisper so the others won't hear.

I try to say "Yes," but my tongue won't move. Paul drops me. I'm surprised to be so near the ground. I hear Paul bellowing, "Brains's hurt. Brains fell down outside."

Brad knows. Guesses, anyway. He stretches out his arm, points his finger at Paul as though there's a gun at the end of it.

Paul says, "He just fell."

I come to in the activities building. My face and shirt are wet where they've been splashing me with water. I say, "Stop, OK?" afraid they'll splash again if I don't speak.

Fat Chuck holds my head up. He says, "What happened?"

I search the crowd for Paul, to see whether his face wears threat or beseechment. It wears beseechment, so I say, "I fell, I guess. I don't really remember." Mark looks at me, knowing I'm lying, but unsure why.

He whispers, "Was it Brad?"

I say, "Fuck you."

94

At the last minute, I fail to shout as I intended, so only Mark and Fat Chuck hear me. Mark puts his hand on my hair, above where it's thickened with blood. He says, "Of course not. Sorry. It's just that Brad's run away. Gone."

In an instant, I know where to and why. I wait for Mark to ask where and why, so I can say, "You'll see," but Mark doesn't ask.

The choir sings "Wondrous Love," which they practiced all week in an arrangement that features one line, then another, so both Ryan's ethereal boy-soprano and Dawn's yeomanly alto shine alone for a moment under the hard stars. I listen, smiling because it's the least painful expression to hold. The room swims less as the hour goes on, and the sickness in my stomach disappears.

Before Discussion Group, Brad appears in the doorway. He's dirty and pouring sweat, beautiful that way, like an animal. We stare at each other, talking, though we don't say anything. They want to ask him questions, but he sits near me and whispers in my ear. In the din, I can't hear him, but I don't need to. I know what he is saying.

Brad ignores the count-off and goes with me because he wants to. Everyone knows by now that we're inseparable, so the counselors say nothing. He presses his side against mine. Heat beats between our shirts. Brad has been running a long way in the dark. Leaves stick in his hair, glittering with sweat and bog damp. Nobody thinks to wash the blood from my hair.

It's the last night at Templed Hills, and everyone is nostalgic. The Tinas have strung up blue crepe paper and written all our names on separate paper plates like fat stars on the walls of a greenish heaven. The girls cry. Porky wins an award as Most Improved camper. His certificate says, "Allen," so nobody back home will know the Porky story. Dawn wins the Shiloh plaque for Christian Witness. Paul gets "Camp Clown." He smiles when he takes the certificate, but you know he wanted the Most Popular, an award that went to Avi the Israeli. It had to be either Avi or Leon, for courtesy's sake, but Paul's disappointed anyhow. He makes a clown face to show he doesn't care. They have invented a special prize for me, for storytelling. It is the best thing anybody has ever given me.

Festivities over, hand-in-hand we troop to the tents, one lantern at the head of each snaking, hymning line.

We sit on the edge of our beds, talking later than ever before, bare legs hanging from bunks, knees rising toward chins on the floor. In the silence between sentences, we hear murmuring voices from other tents, campers talking with friends they may never talk with again, making it last a little longer. Whether it has rained or chilled, whether there have been seven days or one or none, we don't remember, only the timelessness that is at once infinite extension and grievous brevity.

I think it's well that I should be hurt this last night. It is a protest, a rightful symbol. I lie flat, still groggy from the blow. The others sit like stumps in the dark of the tent. I wonder why we don't interrupt each other, since no one can see when someone begins to speak, unless it's Jerry who always begins by gasping and flailing his arms. Communication flows from boy to boy outward toward the hazy summer moon, an electricity of intimacy. Brad's hand dangles from above so close to my face that I feel his heat. If he moves a fraction of an inch, our bodies will touch, but it is not necessary.

Too disoriented for an extended story, I recite a poem my father thinks is funny.

> Ladies and gentleman, take my advice,
> Pull down your skivvies and slide on the ice.

Mark thinks it's funny, too. One of those adult matters, like bitter drink and spicy food. Paul laughs late and loud, imitating Mark.

If I stretch my foot, I hit the suitcase where one clean shirt waits in solitary expectancy. The thought of it fills me with undefinable melancholy. I cry softly in the protecting blackness. I know I'm not the only one.

Gradually, we climb under the covers. Mark does not need to say, "OK, simmer down." Instead he says, "Sweet dreams, men." The murmurs of the far tents hush into quiet so great you hear one beetle pushing in dry leaves under the tent. An owl sits among the branches.

The first sound Paul makes is so uncharacteristic that nobody knows who it was. The scream is like a bird's, high, brief, disorienting. Mark says tentatively into the dark, "Porky?" but the word is obliterated by Paul's second scream, which comes on an inhalation and is, therefore, quieter and more horrifying.

Mark's feet thump to the floor. He's still not sure what or where the trouble is until Paul bellows in his real voice. Mark turns, but the big boy hangs already midair, falling.

Mark's lantern switches on. Other lanterns glitter on the pathway, running to see what the matter is. In the beams, Paul thrashes, holding his ankle. The ankle's twisted and swelling. That must have happened in the fall. It's not the ankle that caused the screaming. Paul's face is red, contorted. Like an infant, he's trying to cry, but no sound comes out. Finally, he forces the word, "Snake!"

Mark shuffles his hand through Paul's sleeping bag. He leaps back, making the gasping sound Paul made at the beginning. From the bag uncoils a black snake, loop after loop, tonguing the air. The lantern light exaggerates its size to black monstrosity, a dragon undulating on the tent wall. It uncoils forever. It drops onto Paul's shoulder, using him as a step onto the floor, whips under the canvas into the blackness of the woods. When the snake touches him, Paul freezes, hypnotized like a bird in a folktale. When the tip of the snake's tail disappears through the gap, Paul begins to bawl, loud.

The Guardian returns to the Temple. The forest leans in, watching.

By now all the lights, all the Tinas and Chucks have crowded into the tent. Each boy's face has its own interrogative illumination, as though by gathering the witness of all the truth might be known. Porky's face in Fat Chuck's light is what one would expect, satisfied, without a trace of pity. Suspicion will not fall on him, though. One advantage of being the fat kid is that no one expects daring. Ryan, with his horror of wildlife, cries too, though at nowhere near Paul's volume. Most of the light rests on Paul, no longer mature or handsome, but a neuter and needy thing, its face blotched with crying.

I can't see myself but assume I look as I feel, a groggy boy jolted out of what was almost a dream. Brad's hand reaches down for mine. It's not withdrawn even when the lights turn on us.

Mark says, "Jesus."

In one of the Tinas' lights, Brad's face floats calm and beautiful, the face of a knight in a legend. I press his hand as tight as I can without the pressure seeping back and hurting my head.

Only one light is left, Mark's. It comes to Brad's bunk. Mark's eyes stare into Brad's a long time, but Brad stares better and Mark turns away. Paul lies whimpering in Mark's bunk, afraid to return to his own. Mark climbs onto Paul's sleeping bag, where the snake was. Even he won't crawl inside. There's a long silence. Then Mark says, "Brad," and not the way you do in love.

In the morning, nearly all the girls cry, waiting and dreading for parents to arrive. Their weeping makes it necessary for the boys to find other means of expression. We jam our hands into our pockets, look at the ground, kick stones. Girls hang around Dawn, in love with her for Christian passions nobody noticed back home. Paul limps on his twisted ankle, pretending nothing happened. He will tell his people it was tennis. He doesn't look at anyone, especially not his tentmates. He suspects no one in particular of planting the snake but sees in it a cabal of faggots and misfits, of a halt and sickening world.

Mark carries Paul's gear out into the sun against the dining hall. I expected the finish to be different. Something was ruined, and nothing whole set in its place.

A small speeding point that turns into Brad's father cleaves the dust in a vintage Chrysler. Everyone gathers around to touch it. Brad is rich, just as Paul said. He introduces me to his father, who shakes my hand like an adult.

"You'll come visit us," he says. He writes the address on a piece of paper and puts it in the pocket of my eighth shirt. He says, "Brad wrote me about you. Thanks for being his friend. It's not always easy."

Brad shakes my hand just as his father did. He seems very tall now, out in the open without trees to alter the scale. I'd be inconsolable if he didn't look miserable, too.

There was a photo of me hoisting a bedroll into the trunk of father's car. My hair lies close, in the Marine butch cut popular with boys then. I am eleven. My sister is five and, to an impartial observer, the focus of the picture, with her curly-haired energy, the ruffle of her small plaid dress in the breeze, the elegantly uncomplicated smile as she watches me lift the bedroll, which, consuming the foreground, seems larger than either of us. Though the photo is in black and white, anyone who remembers the scene colors it with the our red hair, the vivid blue plaid of my sister's dress, the fuzzy robin's-egg of the blanket. The summer sky, too, is blue, but incomparably subtler and more solemn.

The expression on the sunburned visage is at once unremarkable and complicated. A plain child covering up his plainness by making it seem intentional, he makes a face at the camera. Perhaps the lens surprises him midway in a struggle of the spirit so intimate that the invasion is at once unspeakable and unacknowledgable. Only the next instant reveals whether he laughs or cries, an instant, by the turning of the lens onto some other drama, lost forever.

And the night that followed that one was the night of my first poem.

10. GHOSTLY SISTER, PHANTOM BROTHER

Here was the first Tree, the first Sun,
The first and only Child.
And you set out from the circle that was home,
treading the dark round,
crying the strange hosanna in the wild.

WE HAD A SENSE OF HISTORY pounded into us
both by environment and by teachers who seemed different from
now, more intense, at once freehearted and inflexible from the
conviction of right, unburdened by the avalanche of paperwork
and legal culpability that makes teaching today a partially cleri-
cal, partially disciplinary trade. I intensified this historicity by
becoming a bookworm, one of those children who irritate company by sitting in the corner reading the encyclopedia when they
should be affecting an interest in adult conversation.

The life of books is not necessarily more interesting than
daily life, just bigger. It supplies the windy mountainsides, rain
forests, and talking animals that were in short supply in Akron.
Most of what I prized was in short supply in Akron. That's not
Akron's fault. Were I a stranger arriving from some hated home
elsewhere, I would have found everything in the circle where I
was born.

Our teachers shepherded us to the local branch of the public library, to get library cards in heavy yellow paper printed with the image of the winking owl of wisdom. Come to think of it, this was very nearly our first public acknowledgment as individuals. It was not my father's name on the card, not my mother's, but mine. God bless the child that's got his own—anything.

We learned the card catalogue, and Dewey, and to go to the bathroom before going to the library, for the bathroom was kept locked against unnatural assignations, and even to ask for the key involved one obscurely in what one did not understand except that it was too distasteful to be explained. Prizes were given for diligence, parties thrown for those who devoured the most books of a summer, worlds opened, alternatives suggested.

When I was very young, Father read to me under the yellow bed lamp, I reciting the best loved passages in my heart faster than he could read. Sometimes he'd improvise on the text to make it funny. It was the first time anyone bothered to tell me a joke. At one point, the bedtime story hour stopped. This was confusing to me. This was a message from my father, but whether about us or about fiction I was never sure.

The first book I chose on my own was the *Iliad*. People don't believe me when I tell this, but it's true. I remember the day and hour, as though it were the advent of first love. One spring, when light soaked through the windows of the Ellet Branch Public Library in a color between jade and khaki, mother said I could choose whatever book I wanted. I bounded through the green light with library card clutched in hand, the intellectual indenture of childhood over. Deliberately passing the thin bright volumes one knew children my age were meant to choose, I went for the Classics shelf, where a single red-bound book had called to me for as long as I could remember. What Classics were I didn't know. Just that I wanted that book.

Pulled from the shelf, it revealed on its cover a majestic

bearded man leaning out of clouds, head crowned by rays of light. Zeus, of course, I know now, but then a glimmering mystery. The title said, *Tales of the Trojan War*. You opened the cover onto a plate of Odysseus plowing the shore, the squalling form of his son tossed under the hooves of his horses. Another plate showed Achilles sorrowfully lifting the Queen of the Amazons from the dust where he had laid her. Another, Priam bent like an old root in the lamplight of Achilles's tent, begging the body of his son. I read the book a dozen times, besotted, mesmerized. I hid it in my closet so I wouldn't have to return it. I might have it still if my parents hadn't received a call from Miss Apple at the library, at once scolding and understanding. The word "renewal" shouted redemption in my ear. I could keep the book many times, return it, come the next day and have it again.

My daydreams filled with warriors on a windy plain, with the clash of bronze on bronze. I wanted to be part of the story, but my sights were set high. I wanted to be a god, a radiant Olympian, their imperfect but certainly sufficient abilities seeming the answer to all of boyhood's difficulties.

Tales of the Trojan War gave me a mythology in which loyalty, courage, cunning, desperate hope had prominent places. These men fought the way we played our games in Crines's woods. We were Bronze Age warriors in the heart, if aluminum and plastic in actual equipage. Like us also, unfortunately, they manifested deviousness, brag, and violence. The great poem gave me a place where neither my parents nor anybody I knew had ever wandered. The empire of the past was mine, and I chose to live there as often and completely as possible. That this choice could turn out to be problematic could not have been foreseen. Then it was salvation.

To own a book of one's choice was never considered. I assumed the books in our house—Bibles, Dale Carnegie volumes, *Leaves of Gold* treasuries of icky poetry, terrible encyclopedias that used the same illustration for Plato and Moses—had been dealt to us by lottery, and we could neither lose nor add to what was given. When my Aunt Daisy, seeing how I loved to read, offered to buy me a book, I was literally unable to make a selection, torn between joy and confusion, fearing to choose any one book lest the choice close a world to me forever. In the end I took one I didn't want, because it was cheap, and I knew courtesy was honored before curiosity.

Weekly, I haunted the library aisles, filling my arms with mythologies, paleontology and archaeology, lumbering folios of sea life or the animals of Africa, moving through the green light like a mer-child at the bottom of the sea. The library smelled, like the school, of chalk, and one came to associate that smell abstractly with learning. The floor tiles, which, except for the lower shelves, were the architectural feature most apparent to a small boy, repeated the jade of the light, alternating it with a foamy cream that showed scuff marks and which therefore one avoided, hopping like a bird from green square to green square. In this way, I meant to pass unmarked into the adult stacks, having been warned against precocity, believing anything delicious must be in some obscure way illicit.

Before turning eleven, I felt the possibilities of the children's shelves dwindle to the point of desperation. I read everything, reread favorites, resignedly took up unpromising material I'd scorned before. I treated books as though I were a lover and they the beloved. I wanted exclusive use. I wanted them with me, physically, not just as dimming ghosts in memory. I'd been caught hiding *Black Stallion* and *Bomba the Jungle Boy* books behind the furnace so no one else could use them. I continued to keep rare finds weeks overdue, believing I wouldn't love them so much if they weren't meant to be mine. I glanced furtively across the room to the Young Adult section. Some of the titles I could make out, *A Tale of Two Cities, The Lord of the Rings, The Snows of Kilimanjaro,* names that filled me with inexpressible longing, names off-limits until Miss Apple extended the invitation to cross over, until the owl-less drab of the Adult card lay crumpled in one's pocket.

The To Be Stacked cart was sometimes left in a place that could not be seen from the front desk, and on it might lie refugees from the Adult section, page after pictureless page, enticing highways of black print, adventures, whole worlds unfathomed. The fatter the book, the more alluring. I felt free to open the covers of To Be Stacked volumes, but wouldn't actually read more than a word or two, sure that by some librarianish radar Miss Apple would know.

One had to pass through the Adult section to get to the drinking fountain, and then again to get to the checkout desk, over which Miss Apple presided with two-colored walleyes that caught one in a crossfire of accusation should one's own linger too long on forbidden bindings. Nobody minded a glance, as long as it was idle energy and not the premature curiosity children were warned against when they wandered from their Dr. Seuss. I managed to appear to be walking with head straight forward time after time, Miss Apple arranging her wrinkles in approval, until one afternoon when I was arrested irresistibly by a beautiful face.

It was a sad, pale countenance, its hair wild, its mouth so small it might make for singing the singing of a bird. Its enormous eyes possessed a hint of mirth at odds with fatality, amused by, superior to, damaged by all fate. The face comprised the cover of a book on the New or Recommended table. I put down my boyish selections and, for once oblivious to Miss Apple, picked up the book with the sad face on it. Across the spine shone *Shelley*. A girl's name, though the face was a man's. I thrilled at the ambiguity. Through the bindings I felt the vibration of something provocative and intricate, something infinitely remote from the lumpy, familiar horizons of Goodyear Heights. I opened and read:

One, pale as yonder waning moon
With lips of lurid blue;
The other, rosy as the morn
When throned on ocean's wave
It blushes o'er the world:
Yet both so passing wonderful!

I put the book down. With one finger of my right hand, I traced the outline of the beautiful face. With one finger of my left hand, I moved across the contours of my own face, comparing, believing that if, like a blind sage, I could read them out they would be the same. Certainly I was to be a poet. Shelley shouted confirmation. I left my *Golden Book of Minerals* on the table, approached the checkout with Shelley clutched to my chest.

On that day of miracles, there was to be yet one more. Miss Apple did not scold or take the book away. Those librarianly arms uncrossed. Those virgin lips labored into a smile. So radiant was the joy in her skim-milk eyes that I thought she might shout out loud. Perhaps, like Merlin burying the sword in the stone, she had planted Shelley as a beacon to the right soul.

For a year, I loved Miss Apple fiercely.

We ransacked the shelves together for books about Percy Bysshe Shelley. Though Miss Apple enlarged my reach through interlibrary loan, still there was not enough, and weeks went by without undevoured material. I was reduced to fingering the indexes of other books, looking for the magic name, satisfying myself with a line or a chapter or a passing reference. In this manner, I discovered Byron and Keats. I discovered atheism and tourism. I discovered the mother of Frankenstein.

Though I couldn't recall mentioning my obsession, it must have seeped into my speech and carriage, for my classmates, with an indivisible mixture of homage and cruelty, began to call me "the Poet." Eddie Morrison, in particular, couldn't let me pass without using those stinging words, at once so sweet and so humiliating. I had no feeling that my friends knew what a poet was, except someone romantic and withdrawn. Fine with me. I affected a distracted air, gazing into the treetops when a bird sang or the first star glimmered over the ball field at dusk. From the corner of my eye, I saw girl lean toward girl, making words behind her hand: "He's a poet."

Progress is inspired imitation, and I've long since gotten over shame at parading around in what I supposed was the guise of greatness. It was as truthful a gesture as I knew how to make. I didn't know who I was, if indeed I was anybody. But I could be perfectly clear about who I wanted to be.

In the quest for further Shelleyana, I discovered Tennyson and Sara Teasdale and, finally, Edna St. Vincent Millay, who, like Homer years before, announced herself from the shelf, sibylline, drawing my hand across the books to her own volume bound in sea green. She came to mean most of all. A lover of poets, I was not yet a sophisticated reader of poetry. Nevertheless, when I read Millay, even without full sympathy for the adult and difficult emotions, the words sang to me. I stopped loving Miss Apple and began loving Edna St. Vincent Millay. Unable to call her "Edna," certainly not "Miss Millay," I called her "Lady Rain" in my thoughts, for the misty inclemency that formed the typical mood of her verses. I bored everyone to tears talking about her, and then, when I discovered I had bored everyone to tears, shut up about her and let the adoration go inside, where in secrecy it might bear many a strange flower and oversweet fruit.

When I discovered Millay had died the year I was born, I made up a myth wherein I was her successor, the possessor of her spirit. Thirty-eight days separate my birth from her death, and I did wonder a little what spirit inhabited me until hers came in to dwell.

Not until after my reputation as a poet had been established at school did it occur to me actually to make a poem. I knew how to rhyme conventional emotions so to gain praise from my teachers, but I had never attempted true poetry. It took grief. It took the convergence of preparation and occasion, of readiness and incident.

You already know *what* grief, having stood with me in the dirt road of Templed Hills, watching my first hero's car disappear into the distance. But perhaps it is best to forget the particulars. Particulars must, of necessity, disappoint. Say only that it was August, Ohio, the dust thick on the leaves of the Chinese elm. I had closed the door behind me, so grief-stricken there was nothing to do but wait for dark to gather in the windows and hide me, maybe, until confusion might abate. I've always known myself better at night. The moon flowed onto the dusty grass through the dusty lace of the elm leaves. Lonesome and disquieted and bitterly in love, I lacked even the word for what ailed me. I sat in my room praying nobody would knock on the door, praying the house empty, the lavender night full of kindred spirits. A volume of Arab poetry lay open over Millay for inspiration. I would turn from one to the other, Lady Khansa's lament for her dead lover returned to again and again as if in her words I sensed relief for my disquiet. The exhausted green of summer was bleached white by the moon outside the window. Slowly, agonizingly, I wrote. I'd never before felt the power I felt then. I used words that nobody on that street, maybe nobody in that vicinity, ever had since the glaciers retreated.

Before midnight, I'd created a poem. It lay on my desk, white in the migrating moonlight. I wanted to go to sleep and dream of the poem, of my hopeless love, of all that would be available to the tongue of honey I put on that night. I felt the spirit of the poets enter me, as though they'd hovered over the world in the time between their death and my birth, impatient to be reborn. I had given them the vessel. I had given them myself.

It was a putting away of former things. I had a calling. It was a crucial moment in the myth I told myself about myself since the first moment I remember. No—fiercer than that—it was the moment when that myth became visible to the world. If I stood forever on the outside of ordinary things, this was why. If I was left tossing pebbles in the gutter as my pals went off to Little League, if I was awkward and unkempt, this was why. If I had no place and no goal, it was because I had been waiting for this place and this goal to be announced. The poem on the paper said, as nothing had in all my life, *Here I am. Think what you will.*

When I am very drunk, I will still recite that poem.

Whoever says "poetry is not salvation" blasphemes.

Whoever says that writing that poem changed nothing misses the point.

That one becomes one's parents is a fact one accepts after long struggle. The mirror says it, and the parental phrases you hear escaping after you swore a hundred times never to let them pass your lips. One is an ambulating compendium of one's heritage. That my grandfathers and their grandfathers live in me is, now that I am reconciled to it, a comfort. What I want to know is, would the lovers of their youth know them in me? Would they recognize the touch, the turn of phrase? Do I lie the same lies, kiss with the same intensity, sleep with the same soundness? If so, good. The first blood still runs. The paradisal DNA uncoils, a sinless serpent in a sinless garden.

Yet here also is a singular responsibility, one invariably botched before quite recognized. My parents, and theirs before them back to Eve, stood looking over my shoulder that summer night at a halting poem, saying with me, *Here I am. Think what you will.* I was what their labor came to. I, too, became a founder, though of what will be known only after every particular, including my name, blurs into the universal story.

Under the pressure of such expectations, it's important to remember that one need not be triumphant, only faithful. Only willing.

11. THE OASIS OF THE TRINITY

There was an angel of the morning and of the evening,
whether you or I no longer matters,
who came to whom, who descended, who received
crying yes *with open arms.*

I sleep, but my heart keeps vigil.

MY FIRST ENCOUNTER with spiritual matters is almost too absurd to acknowledge. Father has taken me and some of my chums to the East Drive-In to see *Godzilla*. On our own, we have hiked to the Linda Theater to see a triple feature of low-budget vampire movies. I am too young for these things, but I have begged so hard to see them that nobody is to blame for giving in. The outcome is night terrors. I know there is a fanged shadow behind the door. If I move in bed, the miniature Godzilla who's small enough to peer into my window will get me. I cannot walk to the lake at Camp Y-Noah on my own, because of the sea monster, and Father is at first puzzled and then angry that I refuse to fetch the gear we left on the shore. When I finally do get to sleep, I dream of Akron going up in flames, Godzilla wading through the wreckage, looking for me.

This particular night, Mother and Father are going out. Mother is dressing by the pink glass lamps in her room, putting on the perfume I smell now in memory as I type. I am crying. She asks me why, and I overcome my deep inclination to say, "Oh, nothing." I tell her I am afraid.

"Of what?"

"Of monsters."

I think I expected her to make fun of me, but instead she says an amazing thing: "Why don't you pray? Ask Jesus to take the fear away."

I did, and He did. That was the beginning of a life that has been an almost uninterrupted dialogue between me and the long-suffering deity. I have had to keep up most of God's side of the conversation as well as my own, but that, too, has been instructive.

Then, in second grade, I encountered a metaphysical curiosity. Walking home from school—on those days when I took the route I was supposed to take, all the way down Newton Street past the place where the sidewalk bent around the ancient white oak—I was accompanied by a small but dependable convoy of boys. We possessed what might be thought of as a spiritual bent. This sudden fellowship confused me at first, for they lived along Pilgrim Hill and I didn't really know them except for at school, but they were good companions, and we filled up the mile or so with interesting imagination games. Sometimes we'd play Rock and Roll Star. Ricky Thrasher would be Frankie Avalon, and I would be Fabian (whom I didn't know, but who Ricky assured me was somewhat of my temperament). The other boys seemed to be content to be our band. Having assumed our personae, we would strut along in the midst of our entourage, giving attitude, spoiling for a fight, pretending to have elaborate hair.

Sometimes we would play "Oasis," a game which required us to take a flying leap over a ditch or a hedge, screaming "oasis"—

a word we had learned from a cigarette commercial and thought beautiful. There was something mystical about leaping over obstacles and pronouncing the fascinating word, and by universal, subliminal, agreement the game Oasis was preliminary to a discussion of God. Ricky/Frankie generally started it, sidling up to me and saying in the low voice we kept for holy things, "Can we talk about G-o-d?" And if I was in the mood—as I almost always was—I nodded yes. Until we came to Ricky's house on top of Pilgrim Hill, I would hold forth on divine things, and they— to my ever-renewed astonishment—would listen.

I was practicing what could be called speculative theology—which is to say, making it up—but what interests me is my notion that I was enlarging and speculating from a known quality. I never doubted that what I said was true. I was never hesitant or confused. I understood certain things about God, and I was confident that the questions the boys asked me could somehow be deduced and refined out of that understanding. I don't mean to make fun of that understanding by relating it in this way now. I think that what I was saying was basically right—at least close to what I would say now—and derived unarguably from revelation.

No, that's really not the right phrase. Derived from personal conversation with the Holy.

To enlarge on this, I need to I tell you what then happens to me at night. Wind blows the bedroom curtains. I've chosen curtains covered with the shapes of animals, so the shapes move when the curtains move. Birds and dinosaurs and souvenirs of Ohio roadside attractions rattle on the dresser. Marsh smell and tree smell float through the window screens. I hear the noises of real animals from the creek, the long-legged birds, raccoons with bright eyes gleaming. Indistinguishable rustling. There's one midnight jogger. I listen for him to pass, near enough for me to hear his breathing, his footfalls blunted by the summer dust. The hearing makes me happy. I don't want to sleep alone. I want the sounds and the smells of the world to be with me. But I want something more.

Sometimes I fall asleep with the swiftness that is the one blessing I've brought from childhood. Sometimes I determine to stay awake, anticipating the Visitation. Sometimes I choose the night; sometimes it is the Visitor who chooses. Sometimes I fight off sleep so He will come.

When God arrives, the sounds of the night do not go, but intensify, resolving into pure tones, into intermittent showers of distant music. Quietly the roof opens. The ceiling disintegrates like paper in a flash of fire. Stars shine where the ceiling was, less visible than audible, syllables of white fire, voices of deep flame. I wait, coyly, pretending not to want the Visitor as badly as I want Him.

At last He comes. There is not always a shape. Sometimes He is an alteration of atmospheric pressure, a palpable presence in the room, air taking weight and substance, pressing on my eyelids and throat and the tops of my thighs. When there is a shape, He is dark and young, an angel's form, so I will not be afraid. Something in the Sunday School books made me expect brightness, but He is not bright. He is dark and radiant at once . . . I can't explain it . . . another sort of light, that makes radiant midnight and the spaces between stars.

I cannot say how the Presence makes me feel. The closest metaphors are sexual, and yet the experience is not sexual, partially because I am too young to make the connection, partially because there is no *need,* no *wanting* involved. There is nothing to expect, no particular fulfillment to anticipate. I open my arms and receive, having no words for what I am receiving, having no prior experience by which to have wanted it, or to have chafed at its absence. The Visitation is a gift unasked, my reception of it ignorant, spontaneous, totally without context.

I raise my arms, and He lifts me through the broken roof into the sky. I close my eyes and feel the touch of the wind, the pressure of His flight in starlight. I know if I look the regular way it will be spoiled, so I look with my heart. He is not father, not brother . . . He is . . . but then I know if I start thinking too hard, I will change the experience, and what I want is for it to change me. He is not speaking, exactly, but I am hearing. I won't know for days what I am hearing, until someone asks a question to which I know the answer without any reason to know.

I am nestled in the arms of the Spirit, suspended between the worlds. I have known nothing like it since. You have heard it said you don't recover from your first love, and you must believe it.

❄

If your first love is God—

But perhaps everyone's first love is God? If so, someone must tell me, so I can stop dwelling on it.

I prayed deep into the night, though a devout person would scarcely apply the word "prayer" to what I said. It was as lover whispers to lover, asking not for anything in particular, but to keep the conversation up, lovesick, besotted, holding His attention by any means available. I don't know if this is the attitude of a saint or of an animal.

I wait again and again for the dark so I can call to Him. I wait for a time when I am invisible to this world and therefore plainer to His. I watch for the roof to dissolve under the corrosives of the stars. I feel the wind that comes before Him as a sleeve precedes a descending hand.

I have had mortal lovers since. It is not the same.

It is important now, amid the disappointments and compromises of time, to remember that for a while I was blissfully happy. To the limited degree to which I have put this to the test, I discover I am practically the only one I know who will apply the word "bliss" to any portion of his childhood. The ambiguous circumstances of real life didn't matter, not until much later when judgment began to replace inspiration. I am to this day impatient with people who fuss that the PA isn't loud enough or the room is a little too cold, or that lamp shouldn't be *there*. I am still thinking that none of it matters. I am still thinking, *wait until night*.

My own conviction is that the Visitations were external and literal. I don't believe I made them up; the things I would have made up would have been quite different, more gratifying, less surprising. The word "bliss," almost impossible to use in a daily context, covers this circumstance almost alone. Certain nights of mortal sex have come close, but they lacked the elements of personal, radical illumination and change. Sex lacks also the nonattachment, the emotional completeness of a Visitation: never hungry for the next time, ever open if it should suddenly occur.

To spend the rest of life paying for that bliss is surprising but acceptable.

What did the visiting spirit tell me? I don't remember exactly. It was more mood than information. But I think part of it had to do with the fact that there is a level of real activity whose intensity may be mistaken by the unwary for metaphor. A mystic, like a poet, means everything (at first, anyway) literally. I never told Ricky Thrasher how I knew what I knew about G-o-d, but neither did he ever doubt or question me, so perhaps the authority of the source was self-evident.

Some of the feelings the experience left to me have settled over the years into convictions amenable to expression:

I learned that some want to get beyond; some want to get inside. I was one who wanted to get beyond.

Some get beyond by waiting for the next world to flow in around them, like Elfland around the farmer in Dunsany's *The King of Elfland's Daughter*. Some expect to have to beat away. I was among the latter.

I learned that everything is bigger than we think it is. Not necessarily more complex, but bigger.

I learned that, to complicate matters, there is always the fool who cries out, "The Emperor has no clothes on!" when in fact the Emperor is fully and gorgeously appareled.

I learned that heaven is the unforeseen.

I learned that heaven can be taken by storm. It, in fact, in certain cases, *wants* to be.

I learned that the language of experience is altogether different from the language of classification.

I learned that at levels of highest intensity, there is little difference between the ideal and the actual. What difference there is, is grammatical.

I learned that the word is a symbol and that a symbol is a key against which no lock is proof.

I became a poet.

❈

Furthermore, I became a particular *kind* of poet, one sometimes described as "metaphysical" or "spiritual" or even, bewilderingly, "Christian." These titles do not seem to preclude a rather violent physicality, which is also part of my nature. While being introduced at a reading, I heard myself colored as "a man who cannot decide whether to be a voluptuary or a religious fanatic," and though I loved the description, it is quite wrong. I decided, consciously, to be both.

During a quarrel with a former friend in the mail, I experienced her annihilating at once my art and my character with the observation, "You are insensitive because you are a poet, and worse, a 'spiritual' poet, which means you glibly dismiss all human interaction." In part, she was elevating her own craft, the short story, which she thought sprang from and indicated especially acute powers of human empathy ("fiction writers *must* be more in tune with the times than mere poets"), but she put her finger on a partial truth. I never thought that human interaction was the point of my life. Whether this is because I am a poet or just who I am I have no way of knowing, but I suppose, as my bitter friend did, the former. A poet, if he means to be very good at it, cannot judge himself as the world judges him. He cannot even afford to be very aware of what that mundane judgment is. His goal is to please a further audience, one seldom described these days because it sounds so like a fantasy. I have never lifted a pen—or, more accurately, set my fingers on a keyboard—unless it was to establish dialogue with the Holy Spirit. This is one of those things which, in an ordinary context, simply cannot be said. I trust that I'll meet only a fraction of those who may actually read these words, and that their eyes might not have rested particularly on this line.

❀

It is not very surprising to hear a poet declare that poetry is the salvation of the world. I don't even know what arguments I would offer toward a proof, though I am convinced it is true. Cruelty enters when one observes that, unlike a saint, a poem does not approach the wounded soul, but must be approached by it.

But perhaps the proof would include the fact that poetry fuses what rationality would divide. In a time of division, this is a needful magic.

That even faith is corrected by beauty.

That the poet never confuses infinity with oblivion.

It seems to me that, when I was going to school in Ohio, you could say things like "too much or nothing," that you could confide to a circle of friends that you would rather die than not have the life you want, and not be taken for a crazy or a naif. Now, not so. A fetish for proportion rules all. There are pills to cure the extremes of elation and despair, and it is no longer good sense to let poetry take that work on. I don't think it's time but space which has made the difference. A while back, I was reading a critical analysis of, I think, Willa Cather. The writer made a distinction between writers who grew up on the eastern seaboard and writers who grew up on the plains. In New England, he thought, you have the land and the sky, the earthen and the heavenly, to choose as your metaphysical touchstones, but also the sea, tossing and various, a sort of compromise that leads the soul to far places without committing to either the earth or the empyrean. But out on the Plains, there are only earth and sky, only the upward and the downward paths. Saint or voluptuary, or both, but nothing in between. Made perfect sense to me. All or nothing—and if the world says "Nothing," toss in the hand and make it deal again.

Go to the sea's edge. When you stand there, you stand at the point of three firmaments, one of land, one of water, one of burning air, each apparently as accessible as the other. When you step forward, you cannot be sure in which one you will set down.

Alas, but all the Paradises of the West are ruined by the fact that they are defined by whom they leave out. My angry, short-story-preferring correspondent failed to take into consideration that, after a certain point, humanity does not need a just and clear description of its situation. It needs for that situation to be transformed.

12. THE TREE OF LIGHTS

Now I like the rest go grumbling through
the winter streets, hating the crowds,
the cost, the misdirection of it all.
Hating Santa and the hawking elves.
Hating Gabriel for not answering any
of the questions a girl would ask.
Hating Joseph for not calling ahead.
Hating the angels for their cruel salutation,
the golden promise never to be repeated.
Hating myself for growing old.

I HAD A CHRISTMAS TREE this year for the first time in my adult life. I tried a few years back, but the cats, still kittens, annihilated it. I took that for a sign. But this year, a week before Christmas, I was so overcome with the desire to have a Christmas tree that tears started in my eyes when the traffic did not move fast enough, when the local Eckerd's Drugs was out of tree stands, when I could not have the tree bought and up and decorated all in one inflamed gesture. But at last it stood before my fireplace, covered with new lights and new bulbs, and one I had saved from my family's tree long ago. The cats were old enough to sniff a few times and leave it alone. I sat on the couch and looked at it. I was happy. I was so happy. I know it's boring to analyze emotions all the time, but I needed to ask myself why the frenzy to have a tree this year, and why the immense and unexpected delight in having it. I had to tell myself a cycle of stories before I knew.

A friend remembers me saying, "I don't think you can be a poet without being a Christian." I do wish he'd forget that, as he is a Jew (and a poet), and as it misrepresents things on so many levels. But I said it, and must have meant it in some way. Most talk about being a Christian makes me sick, because it is not about Christ at all but about being pleased with oneself. What I must have meant was that I couldn't have found the means to be a poet without some essential story, some eternal myth, informing my imagination—a story at once incredible and thoroughly true, a story that teaches that truth resides on several levels simultaneously, some levels *apparently* excluding others, all variations nevertheless whole and present at once, all functioning, the metaphysical at war with the physical only when you fall into the mundane heresies of *either/or*. A person not capable of eliminating either/or from his philosophical vocabulary, at least in the moment of creation, cannot be a poet. A person not capable of eliminating either/or from his philosophical vocabulary, at least in the moment of prayer, cannot be a Christian. That must have been the connection.

That something might be at once a natural contradiction and an imaginative necessity is the best lesson an artist can learn. And *that* is, additionally, the definition of the Incarnation.

Emmanuel United Church of Christ ("the family church on the hill at Six Corners") was not the best place for a mystic to begin his training. Everyone was reasonable and tolerant and never talked about things like the Incarnation or the Magnum Mysterium. We had a communion of grape juice four times a year. When

I asked once too often who the cherubim and seraphim I heard mentioned in a hymn were, I was told to stop being above myself. On the other hand, perhaps it was a good place to start training, to get the basics, to remember not to be above yourself unless somebody else has put you there.

Never was I more the poet than at Christmas, when I was little, before I had written a single line. Every shred of carol over the radio, every decorated picture window or department store creche was an allegory I unwound with unflagging delight. I was aware of powers in the world absent at other times, invisible forces of tenderness and majesty. Nor was I alone in this perception. Everyone recognized that the plastic doll in the orange-crate creche before the church altar hinted at a newborn god. The three young men of the church who grew beards for the occasion and processed in church-choir hesitation-step down the center aisle bearing macaroni-embossed, spray-painted coffers would be intentionally mistaken for Magi, and yet they *were* the Three Kings long enough for the magic to work.

By extension, I assumed that behind the department store Santa Claus loomed a figure of holy and mysterious intent—Jesus's lieutenant, maybe, who stood in among children, when His own glory would be too terrifying. I took the Incarnation not only seriously but personally. It was not merely an historical event, but Love performing each year a miracle to get one beyond oneself. I was not happy with who I was. Every Christmas was a chance to be otherwise. The chance to be otherwise is the definition of both poetry and faith.

I read legends into each wreath, each carol and twinkling light. Every object, sound, and odor of the season became part of love's allegory, sweet and imperfectly attainable. I thought one was meant to fathom everything by direct contact, as I sometimes fathomed the names of unfamiliar flowers without having seen them before. Without the word "intuition," I possessed the concept, regarding objects of the season as a code left by a god shy as a forest animal, who could be known only by those watchful enough, and persistent.

I walked the tilted streets of Goodyear Heights singing Christmas carols, mostly the old mysterious ones in minor keys that make one feel melancholy and jubilant at once. Down in the rail yards, the trains coupled noisily and comfortingly, muffled by the sheets of snow. I made any excuse to leave the house alone. When my parents resisted, I knew it was because they didn't understand what I was up to, nor how the miracle hung upon my little sacrifice in the cold evenings before Christmas.

Solitary caroling took me farther afield than I'd dare by day. Night was not fearful to me, but protective and enfolding. I believed myself guarded by the sanctity of my task. I was being a poet at poetry's most essential moment, when it is life and not words on a page. My and the world's first poetry was celebration. I gazed through picture windows at my neighbors, at Christmas trees and garlands and twinkling Santas, judging them by some internal measure of joy. I pitied the undecorated houses their alliance with the powers of darkness. The more lights, the more light, I knew, though one red bulb in a wreath on the door was enough to show allegiance.

In school, we'd seen a film about solar eclipses. In one segment, primitives danced and beat drums to drive off the dragon that devoured the sun. Though willing to accept the film's thesis that this was mere superstition, I assumed that even now someone somewhere must dance and drum against the consumption of the light, thereby preserving the world. So I walked the dark streets on cold evenings, singing, not exactly convinced that Christmas came because of me, but willing to serve should it be the case.

Neither solitary caroling nor evening walks were popular in

our blue-collar neighborhood; that I, therefore, had the streets to myself added to the mystique, confirmed my suspicion that powers awful and wonderful focused on me. I must say that, now, with a tone of irony foreign to the actual occasion. Then, the emotion that flooded all my being was gratitude.

I went about with a ledger book borrowed from my accountant father. The pages were divided by a pale green line just left of middle. To the left of that line, I wrote down some aspect of the season—holly, candles, candy, bright-colored mufflers— and to the right, my analysis of what it must mean. My sense of allegory was vivid and undisciplined, as is that of children in general. Like new readers of poetry, I believed that meaning was to be divined by a series of free and fantastic associations rather than by experience. For narrative carols such as "Good King Wenceslaus," I invented plots having nothing to do with the verses themselves, but with the way my imagination inclined toward fables of redemption. I created variations on the knight-in-shining-armor motif, supposing that if a saint could bear supper to a wood gatherer, melting the snow with his footsteps, he could come to lift me from the thralldom of childhood.

Libraries and other adult sources could provide some information, but Christmas was a mystery so holy that nobody knew the whole truth, and, if anybody did, how could he tell it except by pointing to the same things any child could see on the street corner? I sat on Santa's lap, not to tell him what I wanted for Christmas, but to convey to him that I *understood*. I knew who he was and what he stood for. People never ask adults if they believe in Santa Claus, but if asked now I would answer, *yes,* and it would be less a joke than anybody supposed.

All that time I was happy. Presence struck like a strong wind when I stepped into the street, whistling a moment in the cracks when I shut the door on returning home, a patient, mysterious friend unwilling to be sent away. I was the apple of an unblinking eye. Since that time, I've loved night, when it is possible to think of a universe empty of souls but for oneself and the Presence stretched among stars, watching.

The importance of proper decoration of the Christmas tree was absolute and incommunicable. It was a ritual of religious gravity, and one the observation of which would have made me look like a junior league Levite had I not been as covert as a spy, as understated as a fallen needle. Each spun glass ball, each garland, had to be placed just right if the full transformation from the visible to the spiritual were to be accomplished.

I remember clearly the Christmas I understood the meaning of the tree. One evening, as I sat staring with catlike absorption at the shine and twinkle, I perceived the tree was a radiant city. Each ball was the palace of a noble family, the star a rayed cathedral crowning the green mountain. The garlands were horizontal roads, and the hanging icicles vertical stairs and passageways. I adjusted the decorations so each ball would have a garland or an icicle against it, to give its inhabitants a causeway in and out. The tree was a city of light arrayed against the city of darkness outside in the night and cold. The lit-up plastic Santa and the revolving music box Christmas tree in the window became watchtowers, the multicolored houselights on the roof the outer battlements of the city of light. I did not think I was making it up. I believed I was discovering something hidden and perfect. I was inventing history as I had invented theology and allegory before. I composed chronicles and genealogies for the People of the Tree. I could not write them down because they were too holy, and, besides, somebody was bound to ask me what I was doing, and the true answer could not be said aloud, and I would, once again, look like a nerd.

The larger, gaudier balls housed the great families, from among whom the prince of the city and the priest of the cathedral would be chosen. The greatest of the families was the Asters, who inhabited a faceted golden ball with a spiked girdle that made it resemble a tiny chandelier. I'd heard the name Zoroaster and thought it beautiful. Part of my legends of the Asters involved a younger son, Zoro, who knew of the birth of God and tried to convert the city of light but was driven away. I outlined his *Via Dolorosa* down the tinsel and across the garland, to the trunk, the floor, into the dangerous world. Later he returned in triumph, converting temple into cathedral, serving as high priest until lofted into heaven in a burning chariot.

Other ornaments had other histories. If one fell and broke, I wheedled to buy another, not mentioning it was necessary to keep an ancient and noble clan from homelessness. I tried at least to equal their former status, or, if possible, obtain for them a palace still more beautiful. I know this seems a fey and peculiar pastime for a boy. I didn't know, then, whether it was or it wasn't. Perhaps Jesse and Jack and Ricky were all doing the same thing at the same moment, unknown to one another, all mutually recognizing the necessity of secrecy. It accentuated the sense of isolation which may be common to all children, though, of course, I believed at the time I was part of a glorious, silent company.

Where I found myself in this epic is hard now to remember. If, as I suspect, I was the onlooker, the chronicler, then much that happened later is explained. To employ the Hindu parable cited by Yeats, I was the bird that sits on the branch and watches.

It could be also that I was the creator, fashioning a whole world in which I believed so utterly it seemed more a discovery. If so, time and circumstance have made me lose my nerve.

Sometimes, after unjust punishment, after some slight or indignity, in sadness, at the opening of a door and a blast of cold into the room, I perceived the forces of darkness breaking through, and war coming to the plaster Christmas villages. But the city of light would triumph. Imagining that victory multiplied through the homes of neighbors, in all the windows full of light that could be seen from our hill, night after night until

New Year, when the reign of good was assured for another cycle, I spent the holidays of my childhood in jubilation.

Even strangers thought me a happy child. I believe this is part of the reason. The stories I told inside ended with victory. Ended with night and fear going up in flame on Christmas morning.

While my sister lived with her husband in a dangerous part of a dangerous city, thieves broke in and took appliances, wedding presents, table service, and the family Christmas ornaments she inherited by being first to set up housekeeping. It was to be expected. It was the sort of thing that happens. I thought little about it until Christmas the following year. I strolled in the evening when citizens light their holiday lights and joggers puff by exhaling their white mist. Under my breath, so low only I could hear, I sang an old modal carol that made me feel sad and merry at once. Part of my childhood was stolen with that robbery, and yet the loss was so secret it could not be spoken of. Comfort could not even be sought. Who would understand? Who would not say, "Well, go out and buy some more"?

I have, and it is a comfort, yet the loss of the great ornament Houses could be wholly overcome only if I imagined them diffused throughout the dark work, abiding on hundreds of trees, lifting their shields of light against a thousand invasions of dark and cold. Tonight again the powers of light would battle the powers of darkness, and win.

It is almost impossible to write a good Christmas poem. Too much goes into it; it's like trying to funnel a lake through the neck of a wine bottle. For the most part, I have given up straining to get the old feelings back. Instead, I concentrate on the faces of the kids, hoping that their hearts people the twinkling trees as mine did, that *someone* will be walking the dark streets, singing.

13. IN MY FATHER'S HOUSE

They do not know how far
some must go to get to the place
where they started.

I think of a boy's face hidden under pain and doubt,
like some prince, cause lost, waking in exile.

I whisper,
>   I will build it from the ground up.
The lords of the world say there is no ground.
I answer,
>   I will thunder from the sky down.

IT'S STRANGE to enter my father's house now.
Everything is his. What was mine or Mother's or my sister's has
sifted away or receded into closets. This is a sign of health; he
has not let time stand still. The soft face of the kid on the table is
my face frozen in a photo twenty Christmases ago. There are no
pictures of himself. My father, like nature, is a great putter-away
of lost things. I inherited that from him. I have few keepsakes,
few things I wouldn't part from with a shrug. With him, it is
genuine. With me, it is a stance. I keep everything I once loved

inside and invisible, in recognition of the power of circumstance to seize and disfigure. Mostly, I keep words on paper, not merely as keepsake, but as a resurrecting power.

Long ago, my father took me to the Goodyear Tire and Rubber company picnic. I was not a sociable child, and would have found this an ordeal if I hadn't discovered that a crowd provides the most bracing solitude. The peace of wilderness is broken by a truck backfiring half a mile off; once adjusted to a melee, nothing disturbs you. You listen. You watch with what people have described as a reptilian intensity of concentration.

Goodyear provided two festivities a year for the families of employees. One was the Christmas party, where children watched cartoons and received bags of hard candy with green sugar holly at center, and selected free toys from heaps that shone luxuriantly on four sides of the company gymnasium. One year, the prize catch was a home bingo game; another year, a transistor radio shaped like Sputnik.

The second festivity was the company picnic in July, which I loved more because it involved distance and coming home in the dead of night. On the magic morning, we parked on Malacca Street and waited for a bus to take us to Euclid Beach, a giant amusement park uprisen beside Lake Erie, which the company leased for a day so all we had to do was flash Father's employee card and ride anything free as often as we wanted. Food was extra, so one chose carefully and frugally: cotton candy, yes, but never the long pale sausages smothered in onions that only immigrants ate anyway. One might buy a balloon. A cheap one. The best within our range were the double-deckers: a pastel bear head wobbling nested inside a clear plastic globe on a stick, so they could be used to wallop people rather than merely being dragged along behind. Balloons were bound to break or become a burden before the day was over, so one generally opted for wax vampire teeth or wax bottles filled with colored sugar water, whose ephemerality was balanced by the fact that they could be used up before they were lost or discarded.

On the bus, Father introduced me to men he worked with. They were big and happy, clutching the hands of their sons. They wore baggy pleated pants in brown and charcoal, and loose white shirts patterned with pineapples or leaping fish in red or orange, which is what the man of business wore on his day off, the shirt's whiteness proclaiming status, its understated ornament denoting an official state of relaxation. They all seemed to know something about the history it surprised me to have. One could be talked about as though one were a grown-up person.

Father and I did not make alliances with other men and their boys. This was a central fact of childhood. Though our family was not close, it was exclusive. Palling around was not in my father's emotional vocabulary, and though expeditions with other families were not unheard of, they often proved awkward and were abandoned after a few attempts. The fathers and sons on the bus typically traveled in clumps. We traveled alone. This may have been a matter of personality, or it may have arisen from something more material. Father had been struck by polio in childhood. He walked slowly and had difficulty over uneven ground. I didn't notice, but strangers did and learned to leave us to our own pace. When Mother joined us, her bad heart claimed equal attention. Vast chunks of my childhood were spent straining toward destinations that could not be enjoyed until the last member of the party arrived. We were like a convoy crossing perilous waters, proud, cautious, determined to go at our own speed, which, if a pace of delight-destroying slowness, but proved the immovability of our intent.

Walking with such deliberation through amusement parks gave me a lasting peculiarity of perception, which involves close scrutiny of transitional moments and very little anticipation of the goal. To say it another way, out of self-preservation I began to take interest in wherever I was, it being by no means sure that we would reach where we were going, or, if we did that, that anyone would still be interested. I recall few of the rides as keenly and precisely as the asphalted brick roads that ran between them, the sno-cone-clutching families, the smell beside the trash barrels and the oiled machinery of the rides, the boys in white shirts squiring girls in their carnival-colored summer-by-Lake-Erie evening wear.

I wanted to be sixteen and parade around with muscle showing under my sleeve and a girl in a blue halter top leaning on my shoulder. I wanted one of those long immigrant sausages smothered in two-colored peppers. I wanted, above all, to go fast.

When night came at Euclid Beach, the mechanical Fat Lady who rocked back and forth in the niche on the fun house stopped being hilarious and became a little disturbing. Somebody should have shut her off for a while; nothing is that funny. The faces lit by the colored lights became a little harsh. The music of the rides blared a little too loud. The barkers were a little too aggressive. You had seen the same faces too often. They looked at you differently, as if it were time to ask you for something, time to get something that you had and they wanted. I was a kid and had nothing. That would not, perhaps, keep them from asking, from coming to get. When the time came, I was always ready to go home.

❄

Now that I think of it, as a family we were at one point somewhat habitués of amusement parks and county fairs. This marked a change for us, and I think the change was occasioned by my sister, who loved such things. We could use her as an excuse, anyway. When the Summit County Fair moved from the Rubber Bowl to Tallmadge, it was suddenly within a five-minute drive or a half-hour's walk. We went. We watched. We collected the free brochures on well digging and contact with the dead.

Father and Mother were not interested in the sideshows or the booths where you could lift ducks out of the water and win a prize. I was not particularly interested in their apparatus, but I was interested in the people who went there: scruffy, friendly, a little unclean, a little outcast, individuals parents feared but in whom children sensed the almost supernatural kindness derived from the experience of defeat.

Father would observe, "They're always trying to sell you something." He was half right. If he'd gone there in his pleated office worker's pants with the especially rigorous button over the wallet pocket, they would have tried to sell him something. He would have been disappointed if they hadn't. It was different with a kid. I believe they recognized their social function as a life alternative, invariably attractive and invariably rejected except in dreams and B-movies. Everybody planned to run away to the carnival. Nobody ever did. The carnies provided a priesthood of the rebellious alternative, retaining power merely by existing.

On those occasions when I managed to slip away to them, they treated me with kindness I find beyond interpretation even now. The age-and-weight-guessing man shared his evening sandwich of olive loaf and brown mustard with me. The largest-alligator-in-the-world man let me stroke the monster's snout without paying, if only because I said I didn't believe it was real. At the GMC farm truck tent, my friend Ronnie and I were given candy for simply saying "GMC" into a microphone which, we heard with a thrill, boomed into all corners of the carnival. It was our first stab at fame, and I, at least, liked it.

Once, at the Tallmadge Fair, I crawled into the tent of the Fat Man. I hadn't meant to. Father was talking with his friends from the office, and I felt left out. I began to explore. A space of seven or eight inches under the warped canvas let through a strange bluish light. I crawled toward the light and emerged on the inside. It was between shows, and the Fat Man rested on a chair made of railroad ties. The railroad ties were unnecessary, I think, but served as dramatization of the man's Andean bulk. He was staring into the evening blue of the freak show tent, on a platform over a dirt floor covered unevenly by straw and which, I knew since I was so close to it, stank of urine. It was quiet inside the tent, churchlike after the din of the midway. The Fat Man was still and monumental; one who had seen the almost-alive Abraham Lincoln robot at Disneyland could not be certain at first that the Fat Man was real. He had difficulty turning his head, but he caught me at last in the corner of his eye. He said "Howdy" in a normal voice, not a freak voice at all:

"You crawled under the tent."

"Yes."

"Why are you standing way over there?"

"I don't know."

The true answer was that I was terrified. He asked if I was afraid and I said "No," but he knew better. He smiled. He pulled something off the table at his side. He said, "Come over here. There's nothing to be afraid of."

Still fearful, I obeyed. "Fear" is not the right word—holy dread, maybe, such as the ancients felt in the presence of monsters and demigods. In his hand, he held a cheap carnival novelty; if you release the pressure in a paper envelope very slowly, a playing card would emerge as though pulled by magical power. He showed me the trick several times and then gave the novelty to me. My father's child, I tried to pay him, a futile gesture from my empty pockets, which he waved away.

"No. Take it. We're buddies now. Show this to your friends. It will make you very popular. Look what it did for me."

While I practiced the trick, he reached out his enormous hand and touched my head. I understood nothing of compassion and loneliness then, and thank only good upbringing that I did not pull away. In a second, he had dropped his hand and said, "Next show's beginning. Better go the way you came. Remember me, OK?"

I crawled back into the light with the card trick in my shirt. Contrary to the Fat Man's directive, I showed the novelty only to the few and select. The event could not be mentioned to my father, even if he had asked me where I'd got to. Paradoxically, it can—and should—be mentioned to a million strangers.

Poetry is a vocation of remembrance. Poets sit perpetually by an interior campfire, telling the tales of the tribe, which sometimes, but by no means always, are their tales, too. I never wrote because I had "something to say." Always it has been to memorialize. To remember. To insure that the things given to me to love might not dissolve into smoke and darkness. I have been given a sensibility dedicated to the awful necessity of remembrance. It never occurred to me until quite recently to consider whether this is a blessing or curse.

The Fat Man says, "Remember me, OK?" I spend the ensuing years answering *yes.*

The final and encompassing force which makes poetry is remembrance. Without it, the rest is howling, a fist shaken against the wind.

14. GROUND BASS

Ten thousand years a mile-high mount of ice
Sweat in spring a river from its face,
The torrents gnawing pools beneath bare rock,
Melting back and gouging, two pools, three,
A ring of cold lakes built of loosened water.
The streams, like cosmos in a Hindu parable,
Leapt out when night began to dance.

IT IS NIGHT beside a lake. The moon is one paring before full. You are a boy and you want to catch a frog. You know there are frogs in the lake, and that they sing, and that waiting to hear one nearby is your only chance of succeeding before they feel you coming. But you do not know where one will call next—at your feet, at the far side, left, right. Chirpings, thunders, rude gut-rolls punctuate the night. Once you learned how to tell species from species by their sound, but all you remember now is the bass rumble of the bulls, the high chirr of the cross-backed peepers. Sometimes they stay utterly silent. You blame this, probably unfairly, on yourself, on your thumping and crashing on the banks. Sometimes they all call at once, a din of such magnitude the frogs of the moon must hear and answer in their dusty white voices. You take a chance, dipping wildly in the black water. You catch one. You hold it up to the moonlight. A really fine bull, green-black, big enough to poke out of your hand on all sides, neither frightened nor indignant. He calls, thunderously, rapturously, like a tiny explosion, like a harp shivering in your hand. He doesn't know you've got him and doesn't care. All the world is pond and moon and night and singing. You fathom suddenly that the frogs are not really calling; they are being called through. What is more, their message is to you, urgent, beautiful, uninterpretable. Your hand shivers with it.

❋

When I can, I visit the holy places of men and women who loom great in my life: Whitman's Paumanock shoreline, Yeats's Thoor Ballylee and Coole Lake, thicketed meadows in Kent where I imagine Keats might have heard the nightingale. The places where I find joy are those where I detect a resonance between the natural world and the human genius who once dwelt there. Though I know William Blake to be one of the greatest spirits ever incarnate in this world, I can pass his house near London without a second glance. Thomas Wolfe's Old Kentucky Home in downtown Asheville, overlooked by the windows of a giant hotel, is to wave at for the sake of tourists and then walk past. Even as I write, the Wolfe house is a smoking ruin, as though History itself meant to give us a sense of proportion. Milton and Newton may have sat in the same hall in Cambridge, but I am gazing at the brown pictures and the golden architecture and not thinking of eternal genius at all. But where the mind and the planet have danced together, *that* is a sacred place, a Delphi, a mountain-barricaded Lhasa. At one point—standing on the shore of Lough Gill in County Sligo, in fact—it occurred to me that I had holy places, too, and whether others would ever make pilgrimage to them, I should, and soon, while energy is still within me.

Perhaps because I was standing on the banks of another

lake, the first of the sacred places to enter my mind was Alder Pond, in Akron, in the Goodyear Heights Metropolitan Park, which I have called "Maytree" in my thoughts since I was a kid for whom none of the given appellations of the world were good enough. Alder Pond is a remnant of the last glacier. Akron is beset with glacial remnants; you can see at least three glacial lakes just by taking Interstate 76 through town.

The power lines that graze the side of Alder Pond are festooned with miscast fishing lines. It is fed by the sloping moraine northward and drained to the south by the creek that became my first boyhood creek—and eventually the Little Cuyahoga River—when it flows under the Sullivan Street culvert.

I remember when I first saw it. It was a winter evening. People were skating on it. Father was holding tight to my mittened hand. I don't think it occurred to me I was still on the continent that held my house and yard and neighbors. How I knew the glittering flatness I was looking at was frozen water I don't know. Maybe someone had already explained it all. But I was amazed that water so large and wild could exist so close to everyday life. Especially in winter, you can see how the pond lies, at the edge of glacial hills, sunken down into a hollow like an omphalos or a deep eye gazing, unblinkingly, straight up. As time went on I began to recognize that I was drawn back to its peaty bank not just because the Canada geese were so tame they would eat from your hand, not just because you could almost always see the great presiding heron-spirit stalking over in the cattails, not just because you could flip a rock and find a salamander with sides the color of unripe lime, not just because the kids were happy and loud and cast their lines into brown water which, so far as you could tell from the catch, were quite empty. It was because it was a point of transition. The trees broke there, the hills of the park flattened, and water, air, sky, and earth came together at one shivering point. Arrive at morning or at evening, or when the skaters had a great bonfire going in the metal "sala-mander," and you had fire as well.

The pond is approachable from three paths. The right and left paths lead through deciduous forests, with an undergrowth of mayapple and avens. The middle path drives through a stand of pine. As a kid, I attached special significance to this fact, for all the kinds of trees I knew joined at the water that moved my heart. Of course, most of that woods is planted or "new" in historical terms, and the pines downright outlandish. For a person determined on symbolism, these facts do not matter much.

When I first went there, in winter, I saw a low fire under the ice, where the fish and turtles were keeping themselves warm. In later times, I would have explained this gleam to myself as a reflection from the skaters' fires, but I am glad this did not occur to me at the time, for that naive vision allowed me a great truth, that all things are reflections of each other, and if we think any life on this planet is utterly foreign to ourselves, alien or unrecognizable, we need to think again.

I don't think we stayed long at Alder Pond. It was too cold. But I remember it. The best guess is that I was three years old.

I have seen deer in Maytree, and a silver rabbit the size of a dog. I have looked from the top of its great sled-hill and seen the red lights flashing on the blimp hangar, where it rains inside.

I make my pilgrimage to Alder Pond now mainly at dawn, when black ducks and Canada geese stamp the muddy shore waiting for but too proud to beg handouts. I look for the heron, the resident god, who almost never disappoints, but stands statuelike in the shallows, motionless and holy. I look, walk back to the car, hurry on my way. These visits seem abrupt and cursory, but they are not. As with old friends, intimacy can be restored with a word or a glance. With each, I have sunk another root. I know that people seek high places, mountains and towers, so that their spirits can leap into the heavens. Growing up where I did, that option seemed remote and fey. I seek deep places, standing waters, that will lead me down and in.

Ancient music possesses a feature known as the ground bass, a low viol or a harpsichord or male voice keeping a perpetual drone from which the melody lines ascend like sea mounts from the abyssal plain. The Aboriginal didgeridoo and the chanting of Tantric monks provide such a ground bass. My own singing voice is bass with a serviceable high range. Most singing is physically pleasurable, but when I am required to rumble along at an A or the bottom G or on to the notes below the bass staff, the pleasure is intense and difficult to define. Perhaps "erotic" is the word, or in Oriental terms, *yang* to the limit. I feel I've caught a note sung by the depths of the world; all that is necessary is to open my mouth and the fullness of things floods out.

Tibetan monks, when asked how they manage to sing a triad, answer that they do not. God sings it through their throats. I've tried it and do believe it cannot be done without supernatural assistance. The effort did pay off in the ability to hum and whistle at the same time, a talent which has some cocktail party currency.

The urge to get in and under is in me subservient to the urge to get out and over; it is, nevertheless, there.

Visiting my hometown now, I find myself in places I never dared when I was a daily resident, places only the curious stranger can go without social implication. On one such visit, I wandered downtown, where the cycle of construction and demolition revealed a city hidden throughout my youth. Under the streets of Akron, the canal still runs, much of it bearing dry air, subterranean, gliding in green-black silence, empty in places, shivering with black still pools in others, through arched catacombs scarcely imagined by me when I was living there. I suppose all of this must have been there, maybe it had even been visible, but people like *us* never went south on Main much past the corner of Exchange Street. I couldn't tell you why. Like lions sniffing the sign of another pride, we knew, even in extreme youth, without being told, that there were some places it was no use going.

There, under the wrecks of buildings just west of Main Street, in the shadow of the old Y, I saw the gliding V of a muskrat in the still black water. I have told any number of people this and have received arched eyebrows in return. The editors of this very book red-pencilled the passage with some vehemence, explaining that people who know about such things find the place I describe unplaceable, the gliding of the muskrat hugely improbable. Nevertheless, I have seen what I have seen. I expect to stand on the spot and show everybody what I mean, but if that should not happen, if I should return to South Main and there be nothing but the rows of buildings apparent in my youth, I will assume that, rather than having made a discovery, I have been vouchsafed a vision.

My muskrat's life must be one of the most secret in the world.

If the city were abandoned tomorrow and only these hidden arches remained, buried, then revealed by an archaeologist's spade, people would mean them when they said the ancient, half-forgotten word "Akron," not knowing that no more than one percent of the people living there ever saw them. If I were to sit down and write the story of a life—any life, God knows, mine—I would be writing practically nothing that was a daily concern of my subject. Honors, achievements, calamities roll off and into the darkness, and every day the city wakes up and goes to work, each one of its people waking with it, filled with the dark waters and secret passages, with visions they have scarcely dared to tell.

Like the warble of a toad or the roar of oceanic breakers, ground bass implies depth greater than what is heard, greater than what is hearable. If I were a philosopher I would determine that the ground bass is the motive principle of the world, at once firm and fluid, underlying and pervasive, the apotheosis of matter, the vibration of the elements themselves in the wind of the spirit. The central Stuff. The notes of the best poets when they sing with their throats wide. The Throne of God: pure matter, matter concentrated to the density of a collapsed star, matter sinking out of this dispensation into dispensations unsuspected.

Why do we associate divinity with the ethereal? Why not with the unimaginably material? Why is God on high? Why not God in the Deep?

If there were a wave-conducting medium between us, we would be able to detect the musical pulsations of the sun, deep beneath all plausible scale. Pythagoras knew that the arrangement of the planets is rhythmic and melodious, and looped the strings of a lute from planet to planet to Delphi. The stars sing. The atom sings. From whom else did the poets learn it at the Beginning?

Contemporary physics contemplates the ground bass just as the mystics of old, though it uses different terminology. Its term is the "quantum vacuum". The quantum vacuum is not a vacuum at all in the classical sense, but an array of possibilities, like a movie screen before an infinity of projectors, upon which practically any image may be thrown "spontaneously" at practically any time. The quantum vacuum is a cauldron boiling with potential. Timothy Ferris writes in his book *Coming of Age in the Milky Way:*

The quantum vacuum is never really empty, but instead roils with "virtual" particles. Virtual particles may be thought of as representing the possibility, delineated by the Heisenberg indeterminacy principle, that a "real" particle will arrive at a given time and place: Like the pop-up silhouettes on a police firing range, they represent not only what is but what *might* be. As quantum physics see it, every "real" particle is surrounded by a corona of virtual particles and antiparticles that bubble up out of the vacuum, interact with one another, and then vanish, having lived on borrowed, Heisenberg time.

The upshot of these virtual particles' flashing about in the quantum vacuum is breathtaking and so "poetic" one suspects that physics is somehow in the poets' hire.

There is no longer the need to decide where the universe came from. Given the fullness of time, the emergence of something—even a great deal of something, such as a universe— from nothing is perfectly expectable. Ex nihil. Physicist Edward Tryon states categorically that the universe is a "vacuum fluctuation." The Greek philosopher Anaximander said much the same thing, that creation is a sort of glitch, an "injustice" in the serenity of *apeiron,* the infinite indefinite. A Hindu might call it the starting up of Brahman from timeless sleep. A Western mystic might say it is a rhythm suddenly above the rhythm of the ground bass, a counterpoint, a harmony. One might simply call it *inspiration.*

A controversy in which I am frequently involved in my present vocation as college professor has to do with valuation of the canon. I believe that some works of art are better than others, and that this judgment is—finally, though not initially—objective, and that all honest and informed minds will eventually reach similar conclusions. Most of my colleagues do not believe this. I am in behavior such a rebel I am surprised to believe it myself, so Platonic, so hierarchical, so unlike me in my daily activity. I realize also that my determination of what is eternally great is not wholly rational, but involves a frisson, a vibration I will accept as emotional, but which I judge to be bodily. Apprehension of the greatness of a great poem or a great painting or a monumental work of architecture is so *material,* so like a blow to the chest I assume it *is* a blow to the chest, an emanation arising from the true quality of the thing perceived and not from my "taste." Indeed, this thump in the solar plexus often contradicts my former taste. I believe I have, like a scientist, felt a real power in real objects, though I have no way of reproducing the experiment, as my colleagues, unlike scientists, love and sanctify their prejudices rather than seek to shrug them off. If I suggest to colleagues that so-and-so really isn't very good, even though she's a black woman, I have done a trespass that has nothing to do with so-and-so's real qualities as a writer, but rather with the way my colleagues have chosen to look at the world.

I have always wanted science to adopt the vocabulary of art, which is to say, the vocabulary of wonder. I believe that art criticism can adopt the patient selflessness of science and look at the *thing* rather than at its own dear self looking at the thing. We can resign ourselves to hearing the ground bass, to feeling the vibration, even where we have willed it not to be.

Once, at Hiram College in Ohio, I taught English composition in a chemistry lab. I liked the sturdy black tables, the faucets and gas nozzles, the variety of playthings unavailable to the mere humanist, the acrid smell of scientific enterprise. On the wall hung a copy of the Mendeleev/Moseley periodic table of the elements. I faced the periodic table; the class faced me. By the end of the term, though I've no idea what they learned, I had memorized the elements, their numbers, families, weights, symbols. Unheard-of astatine. Comic book krypton. Unlikely yttrium. Jaw-cracking dysprosium. Unpronounceable unnilquadium. Incorruptible gold. Hydrogen the Founder. Plutonium the Destroyer.

Regarding the particles of the chemical world, I was troubled with questions of purpose. Did exploding stars know they were making osmium and mercury? Would they have thought their expenditure repaid? Was hafnium part of the divine plan, or did it merely appear as debris after some more central labor? Are there somewhere tossing seas of niobium bound by bismuth dunes gleaming in the light of double suns? Life forms based on cobalt as we are upon carbon? If not, why should cobalt be at all? Do the souls of the elements not aspire? Is there a universe sprung from each of the elements, as ours from hydrogen? Is thulium the ur-atom of some creation undreamed of, a table of elements branching from it of unimaginable complexity, whose very winds are lead? I repeated the polysyllables to myself while my students bent over their compositions, those oceanic words never said in ordinary human discourse, the glowing inert halogens, the brittle metals, the everlasting rare earth poisons.

I realized my obsession was partially a gesture of disapproval. I knew what the table was for, but also that the whole enterprise was a needless elaboration on something more elegant, and in the spiritual (if not quite the chemical) sense just as instructive. Out of all this, what is necessary for a man to know is that the universe is nothing if not various. Take one neighborhood, Jupiter and its satellites, and you have what appears to be a prodigal and unnecessary abundance. Worlds of ice. Worlds of fire. Worlds vomiting sulphur. Worlds exhaling metallic nitrogen. Worlds smooth as a baby's bottom. Worlds tormented. Worlds writhing like Milton's Pandaemonium. What is the point? That the Almighty stoops to bravura? That electrons rise to it? That all these worlds are variations on a limited number of themes but makes them the more staggering. The greater the artist, the more he does with less.

In the fifth century before Christ, Empedocles of Acragas asserted that Being is fourfold. In other matters he seemed to have followed the party line of his fellow Eleatics: that 'that which is' logically can never be 'that which is not' or 'that which will be' or 'that which was.' Being is being, uncreated, indestructible. This is very Newtonian—or rather Newton is very Eleatic. We call it conservation of matter and energy. We get nervous if it doesn't lurk somewhere in our cosmologies. Contemporary physicists who flirt with the assertion of creation ex nihil assume that nihil was once *something*—a black hole or other singularity—in another universe. Poets find all this quaint, lacking one bad intellectual habit scientists possess: we do not become obsessed with the logical extremes of even our most cherished principles. Always-was-ness does not seem to us to be a necessary, or even a logical, adjunct to Is-ness. Sometimes-not-being appears a perfectly expectable quality for being to possess. Who made you believe that 'what is' is any guide to what can be? We are bored by questions like, "Where was God before there was a universe?" because they are immaterial and therefore unpoetical. When a poet is told about chaos science, his response is "Yes, of course. Whoever thought otherwise?"

The physicist who wishes to complete her cosmology consults a poet or becomes one herself. Much has been written of the futility of poetry in contemporary times, most of it beyond contradiction. But rather than a body of poems, it is the habit of poetical perception which will prove necessary to the visualization of the coming world. Poetry is like the discarded stone of the canticle, thrown away today to become the cornerstone tomorrow, or like those forgotten Greek texts moldering in Irish monasteries and in the saddlebags of wandering Arabs which would one day remake the world.

Poets borrow the discoveries of science while pitying the pace and caution of these discoveries. The central labor of science is to compact the Enormity, to keep a lid on the universal conflagration. The poet whispers, "Let it burn."

15. GETTING DOWN

Grandfather fire is in us. Grandmother, the abiding.
We reach out and take. We have
turned winter into world again.
We fetch this hill from nothing.
God howls and we suck him down.

MY SISTER used to dig. I know when it started, though not exactly why. It began when father taught her to dig for earthworms in preparation for fishing trips. Why it went beyond that is anybody's guess.

Father kept his tools in the garage. By standing on a wooden stool, my sister could lift the garden spade from its hook on the garage wall. She would drag the spade across the grass to the empty lot on the far side of the street. Why there? The compass point is southeast of our front door, if that meant anything. It was the flood plain of Roosevelt Ditch, if that meant anything. Site selection was as mysterious as the reasons for the entire enterprise; one could but stand and watch.

She marched to the site, dragging the heavy tool across the ground behind her. The first task was to chop away the overgrowth. Teasel and Canada thistle and sow thistle and hairy lettuce and tough wild grasses had their stems frayed away from under them. She scrapes a bare spot with the side of the spade.

Once the ground is clear, she begins to dig, needing to jump on the metal rim with all her weight to open the glacial clay.

After the first day of digging, there is a noticeable depression in the meadow. After the second day, the hole is deep enough to twist an ankle in. By the fourth day, one waits until she goes indoors for the evening. One creeps out to peer over the brink and look. She has labored so long and diligently there must be something wonderful at the bottom. I go. I look. I see dirt. But tomorrow she will be there again, digging, heaving the dirt out with a spinning gesture she invented herself, which sometimes lands the dirt back in the hole but gives it a fine plumed effect wherever it goes.

Sheer will gets her through the first layer, tangled as it is with roots and corms and leathery tubers. A fraction of an inch farther down lie the roots of trees, some attached to living specimens fifteen feet away, some the remnants of what was cut to make this field. She will dig around the thicker roots until she has room to swing, then hack at them with the spade edge as though it were an axe. She is small but durable, and she prevails.

Red worms and white grubs are the main fauna in the hole. She gathers them if she intends to go fishing, rolls them gently to the side if not. Opportunistic blackbirds hop about in anticipation of morsels.

The dirt she spins over her left wrist is the richest in the world. Drained, it will grow anything. It pushes out wildernesses of willow and great ragwort. It lies five inches thick everywhere and, in places, six times that. Out toward Hartville, the loam is so rich and airy it burns. This miracle underfoot should be shouted from every pulpit, spoken aloud at the start of every TV newscast, in thanksgiving and amazement.

A little deeper and the black soil becomes gray-black clay. The land lies low and wet, without significant burrowing animals, and the clay gleams like satin, like a fine pale chocolate. Water seeps from it at a touch. Now and then, my sister strikes red-gold stones flecked with mica. These are the low hills of Canada splintered by the ice sheets and carried to our vacant lot. Few appreciate this gift brought over so much time at such an expenditure of labor. My sister hacks at them until they shatter, her small energy focused into more damage than the glacier did in a thousand years. If they are too big, she goes around.

Ancient hardpan is next, though she doesn't often get that far. She goes out one day to find her pit filling with water, though the creek is fifty yards away. She empties it with a bucket and keeps on digging, believing somehow that she can get beneath the water. Perhaps she can, but I can't tell her how. Finally, she has to abandon the dig. Even the flooded pit is of some interest. Algae and water striders appear magically, as though they'd hid in the soil waiting for a pond to come to them. Camouflaged with goo and plant detritus, the surface is indistinguishable from the face of the soggy meadow, and sooner or later someone will be tricked into stepping knee-deep in silvery ooze.

I like the pits best when there's water in them, at which time my sister tacitly wills them to me. I crouch over them, watching the sky move across the dark water. She turns to other matters for a while, but inevitably one will hear in the garage the scraping sound that is my sister climbing to the spade hook.

If she could just keep going—what? What does she long for that is unavailable in the light of day? Agate, turquoise, emerald? Lizards that lived before the cold? Bones whitening where ground sloths and titans and rebel angels lay down to die? The Nadir studded with black suns. The Hand open at the top to give, open at the bottom to receive.

If it were possible to get deep enough, my sister would have done so. An angel would have given her a shovel to outwit the waters, a charm against salamanders, a balm against the fires at the center of the world.

The spade hangs where it has always hung. Nicks and dings caused by my sister's attacks on the jetsam of the glacier have not been polished out. It is largely at rest. My father uses it to dredge the ditch or uproot frostbitten tomatoes before winter. Its former glory is not generally recalled. Last year's dirt crumbles from the juncture of handle and head. Like the scepter of a king used to prop a peasant's door, it can be mistaken for an ordinary tool. If, as I suspect, things gain souls and consciousness through contact with our souls and consciousnesses, then the spade spends its time thinking, remembering, trying to imagine where it was going those years ago when my sister kept it pointing in and deep.

❄

What is the dream of the secret places?

At once to be opened and to be left in secret.

❄

I met my niece, Rebekah, my sister's daughter, for the first time when she was two. She'd been born while her parents were serving as missionaries in Pakistan. A bright, verbal child, she reminded me of her mother at the same age. Left to his own devices, her brother Jonathan, a year older, runs like a gazelle, like a wind blowing. He is airiness personified. Left to her own devices, his sister Rebekah crouches by open ground, digs in with her bare hands until she has a bare spot, a hole, a growing chasm. Her interest in the excavation seems boundless. If one looks where she was looking, one sees a hole in the ground. One understands from the intensity of her scrutiny that this is not what she was seeing at all. Invariably, someone catches her and drags her off to more intelligible pastimes. I watch, transfixed, finding it difficult to decide which of two moments, which of two down-digging girls, identical though separated by thirty years, I am witness to.

Accidental death was nearly my lot on three occasions in childhood. All involved water. Let one stand for all: my father and I are at Camp Y-Noah, on an Indian Guides weekend, during which the festivities included the building of model boats which were powered by rubber bands driving a balsa wood paddle. My rubber band had flown loose all at once, leaving my boat stranded in the green lake. I reached out from the dock to retrieve it and fell into the water. I must have twisted around, for I saw a whirlpool, green-white, like the most precious jade, dancing above me, marking my passage with some dispatch to the muddy bottom. One of the fathers dived from the dock and rescued me. Back on the dock, I spluttered and dripped, but I remember everyone remarking how I didn't seem to be afraid.

I wasn't. It had been beautiful.

Though I always loved the water, it took me a long, agonizing time to learn to swim. All physical tasks came slow to me, but in the matter of swimming there was something more. It was a breach, a violation, like a prenuptial agreement getting in the way of true love. To learn to swim was to be separated forever from the power of the element whose possession I believed I was. In my adolescent Percy Shelley phase, I read of the poet lying ecstatic on the bottom of rivers, enraptured by the depths, swiftly drowning until one of his friends beat down to rescue him. It was then that I finally learned to swim. If people thought that this was a way to avoid the water, they were mistaken. It was a way to get deeper in.

A tarot card reader told me I am "the air of fire." An astrological friend discovered that my sun is in Virgo, my moon in Taurus, with Libra rising, and that enough of my planets reside in earth signs to explain at once my solidity and what one would probably call my earthiness. In my own perception, my element is water—the bright surface that stopped my sister's search. I long for the thing that blocked her way. I begin to make a parable of this. I stop, realizing this is what I *would* do, watery one, happy to flow around, surround, outglitter, leaving it to others to sound the Center.

16. ROOSEVELT DITCH

I will tell you how to stave off drowning.
Make sea taste you are a stranger,
a struggle, an anomaly: the salt of weeping
amid the salt of the crumbling world, twice bitter.

Make it no longer worth his while.
Make him think twice.
Make him slam the emerald door.

THALES OF MILETUS, seven hundred years before Christ, believed that all things were water. It was the pervading and essential substance, an underlying and immortal changefulness. Though since superceded, Thales's conclusions were not unscientific. When he speaks of the Absolute, he speaks of the moist, not of the god of water, a step one might think of as ambiguous but which, nevertheless, leads in a straight line to the modern world and its cult of objectivity. Thales presumed that a single order underlies the chaos of human perceptions, and, furthermore, that we are able to comprehend that order. Thales looked at his environment. He saw water falling from the sky, flowing from rock, oozing from plant and animal life, encircling his little town on the coast of Asia. He knew that water alone, of all things visible to the naked eye, takes on all the physical manifestations of matter—solid, liquid, gas. He observed that bulbs and tubers lay dormant in the dry Mediterranean soil until the advent of the winter rains, that human and animal babies came forth into the world from a cell of moisture. If water appears to be in all things, perhaps it *must* be in all things. Perhaps it is the First Principle itself.

Given time, I would have thought of this myself. Water is the element for those who are not ashamed to have been made, those not terrified of the ultimate unmaking. I want to say, "The mind of the poet is water," though I fear the chorus of earthen and airy and fiery poets who would thunder otherwise. My mind, at least, works like water. Stymied, it settles in, goes to sleep, turns to other things, and in the morning, after not thinking of it at all, finds itself on the other side of the obstacle, exactly where it wanted to be. I take no credit for this. It is an innate fortune.

The Tao is like water and I am like water, and if the Tao is as oblivious to itself as I am most of the time, then truly am I saved.

March. Rain and thaw. Flood time.

We lived south of Eastwood Road. To the north lay the Wildwood. There, two hills and a tilted plain surround a marsh. The eastern hill was farmland abandoned during the Depression, having had time since to grow up in hawthorn and a wilderness of monstrous black willows. Caney and briary, this country was almost impassable. Where you didn't sink, you were slashed. Where you weren't slashed, you passed within sight of the windows of the owner, who was rumored to go to any length—to the point of homicide—to insure her privacy.

The graceful nineteenth century farmhouse on Darrow Road had long since crumbled away from neglect. The end began when its owners sold the land across the road, not suspecting it would become a drive-in theater and a drag strip, roaring of engines by day and the tinny voices of movie stars by night.

For a while, the ruin served as the regional haunted house and love tryst, until vandals torched it into its own foundation. By the time we moved out of Goodyear Heights to Eastwood, I was the only boy my age much interested in roaming around. I discovered everything myself, corroborating later with boys who had grown up there and known it of old.

A rich man bought a low, boggy quarter of the property, built a horse ranch, and dug two large ornamental ponds. After a locally famous divorce, his wife became the chatelaine. She was jealous of her privacy. She shut herself and her willows and her mosquitos behind fences and guarded all with a scowling groundskeeper. These were not hindrances to the determined. We climbed, prowled, spied, our hunter's alertness serving us like Pluto's helmet. Besides, if the groundskeeper were scowling, he was also handsome in a brooding Heathcliff sort of way, and we told each other bawdy melodramas about what went on nights behind her forbidden windows.

Summer evenings were sharp with the crack of the groundskeeper shooting snapping turtles out of her ponds, after her silly white ducks had disappeared one by one, each in its swirl of startled blood. The groundskeeper was indiscriminate in his slaughter, and each summer we begged permission to come in and capture the nonsnappers and bear them to safety. The rich woman was more interested in privacy than ecology, and she refused us. Perhaps the groundskeeper was more interested in target practice than ecology, and the refusal came from him. Through the culvert that poured under Eastwood swirled bits of broken shell and darkenings of the brown stream we took for reptile blood.

The western boundary of the marsh was a hill of virgin forest, uncut but certainly not inviolate, a crown of beeches on a brow covered in spring with violet and veronica, high, dry, clean as parkland under the limbs of the silvery trees. Everything was silvery. The dirt lay silver under the rocks, clean as sand. Even the rusting chassis of abandoned cars and farm machines maintained a clean-limbed grandeur, Attic in their derelict simplicity. The trunks of the beeches gleamed silver by night, satiny white by day.

In the shade of the beeches lay the Hill of Burials, where we interred dead puppies and Easter chicks and such road kills as we were able to touch without our mothers seeing. We chose the place because of a conviction of holiness that communicated from child to child without our ever mentioning it aloud. Remembering the Hill of Burials makes me think of the phases of life which, like light, are two things at once: both a continuum and a series of episodes never fully to be understood, never to be repeated—a long wave and a changing dance. On days when a burial was necessary, I never felt more removed from my parents and the world around me. My grief would be incommunicable and beyond comfort. Elders would think it absurd to be in this state over a kitten or an Easter chick. They would want to dig a hole in the garden and be done with it. I understood their point of view but felt they did not understand mine. They grieved over old ladies at church and distant uncles tottering off to their rewards. I understood that. It was given to them. It was their service. This was mine. I hid the tiny corpses in the pocket of my sweatshirt and set out for the Hill of Burials, not daring even to take a shovel, knowing from experience that a sufficient grave could be dug with the boot heel and bare hands. I would pray over them until I had a vision of them in heaven, happy puppies, cheeping chicks scampering over a field of light.

At intervals throughout the year, a patch of raw earth would signal a small tragedy brought there in silence and with as near as anyone comes nowadays to natural religion. I suspect this is how the holy places of antiquity were selected, by unanimous and mystical consent.

It is difficult for me to enter that room of my past now. But I don't disown it. Though I must now think of those activities as a little embarrassing, I long for the absoluteness and equality of the convictions we acted upon, that good must surely happen if the world is left to its own devices, and even to the least.

The flood plain tilts northward. If you'd walk straight, you'd hit Lake Erie through the eastern suburbs of Cleveland. It would be laborious, as you'd be fighting the east-west grain of the land. "Groove" might be a better word than "plain." In former times, it was the bed of the Wisconsin glacier. Ice loomed a mile high over the cattails, the grinding weight of it hollowing a depression that still retains water and spills Roosevelt Ditch southward across Eastwood Road into Akron, through my father's backyard and the backyards of all our neighbors, toward the Little Cuyahoga and the Cuyahoga hairpinning back toward the Great Lakes and the Saint Lawrence and the seal-haunted North Atlantic. Standing on the banks of the creek, you were a voyager and an explorer. Touching the water, you were touching all the North.

All life goes to the water. Come down to drink. Build your cities there. Ur and Benares and Memphis.

We called Roosevelt Ditch "the creek," as if there were no other. We overturned its rocks for crayfish. Nobody told us how to do this. We just knew. In computer parlance, it was part of our hardwiring, an inheritance from hunter-gatherer fathers at the dawn of time. Should we ever, after the Holocaust or some natural calamity, need to become hunter-gatherers once again, we'd owe what skills we have to the creek.

If you went down at morning, you'd catch herons and muskrats at their work. You'd find the spoor of foraging raccoons in the black mud. If you followed the creek bed southward, you came to look-alike developments where newly wed factory workers set up housekeeping behind pink and yellow aluminum. They sat on their back stoops at evening, their diapered babies crashing to a stop to watch you pass with your jar full of the frilled creatures of the creek rocks. The houses stood far enough from the water that you could get nearly to the Newton Street culverts before you had to pay attention to civilization.

If you followed the creek bed northward, you came to the marsh I've just described. We lived near the source, a blessing I understood even then. Elderberries and gooseberries throve in our yard. Frogs forayed out of old habit. Cowslips bloomed in the first of spring before the lawn mowers finally discouraged them. Hideous phallic eruptions of skunk cabbage bent the earth back before the snow was gone. The creek was used to owning the land.

If you watched long enough, you'd encounter the Creekers, boys whose obsession with Roosevelt Ditch was greater, or at least more material, than mine. There were the big Tallmadge boys who knocked at our door at breakfast with the mist around them and empty muskrat traps dangling from their shoulders, telling my mother that they knew I hung out in the swamp and thought that I had been springing their traps. It flattered me to be accused by them, though, in actual fact, I didn't know until then what a muskrat trap was. Afterwards I *did* know, and sprang them with stones or sticks as soon as I found them, the boys' accusation turning into prophecy. Never accuse the innocent. It gives them ideas.

On a shoulder of the hill of the silver beeches lay a pond left over from the Darrow farm. It marked the intersection of a dirt path that descended from Darrow Road through a double line of apple trees, and one that wound up from Eastwood through plowed fields. It must once have been the farmer's main route through his fields, for it was wide, deep, surviving decades of neglect. Coming or going, he would see his pond. It nestled in the prow of an artificial plateau, so you could stand on its bank and look half a mile in any direction over the marsh. People who'd lived long in the neighborhood recalled dairy cows ambling to drink the blue-green water. Older sisters of my friends remembered having to come home when cowbells signaled their slow ascent to the milking barns. They were adults before they realized the phrase "when the cows come home" was meant as hyperbole. From the air, the pond would have made a nearly perfect oval set amid deep banks, with one graded and trampled side where the cows came down.

Amazing how much adventure we got from a shallow pond even a girl could toss a stone across. Sometimes there were swimmers, though it had to be early in spring before the scum blossomed in force. I was a very young boy when I saw a man swimming, and, yet more amazing, when he walked from the water, the dark hair on his chest and legs and crotch. Had I never seen a naked adult before? If I had, I must not have noticed. I wondered if he were another race, another species that he should have such bizarre ornament. I did not see him go into the water, but I saw him come out. Had he arisen there? Was he a merman? Was he one of the gods I read about in library books? My wildest surmises were confirmed when I tried to share the moment with my mother and was told she did not want to hear about such things.

The pond was sufficient to fish in. I caught a huge catfish once and, later, a perch big enough to eat. We did eat the perch, but the catfish got put in a cement fish pond that my father built in our backyard. My guess is that the catfish is still alive, though the cement pond vanished long ago.

Once, my sister hooked a gigantic turtle. It was not a mere reptile but an angelic power rising black and terrible from the depths, a daughter of the World Turtle whose back we ride through the zodiac. The nylon line broke as she was hauling it onshore, while just head and rim of midnight black shell broke water. I was content to leave it be, in holy dread, but my friend Jim decided it could and must be caught. In deference to its hugeness, we took a hundred feet of clothesline and baited it with ham and left it slung across the water overnight, anchored at the ends with tent pegs. In the morning, the pegs were pulled, the ham gone, the clothesline snapped in two dead center. We postulated a pit deep as the world at the pond's center; otherwise, there was no room for such a monster.

The turtle must have remembered the farmer and the muddying feet of the cows. The turtle may have climbed up from the swamp before there was pond, or farmer, or white house on the hill. Though it is almost too much to hope, the turtle may have lumbered away before the bulldozers came, and lies, huge and undefeated, in some deep place still.

Occasionally we could get someone's father to come fishing with us, which meant we could stay deep into the evening. I loved it then, the bats fluttering over in a sky of flamingo and murex. The pond grew darker without ever quite disappearing, a blue-silver mystery with your friends standing at the edge, disturbing its calm momentarily with their baited hooks and voices. I was the only kid not much scared of the dark, and I took advantage of that by creeping away into the shadows, emerging behind my friends and letting out a banshee shriek. This was not an endearing habit. The woods trembled with fireflies, the bearers of the lights invisible and, therefore, vulnerable to an infinite speculation. When I read of fairy lanterns in stories, I knew instantly what was meant, and how someone could follow them until the way was lost. At a certain depth into the forest, the wolves began. Beyond that point, none of us would go. Not on a dare. Not for any money. That we knew in a schoolroom sort of way that there were no actual wolves did not matter in the least.

My sister was the most successful fisherman. This was because she desired the fish most. I usually felt disgruntled at actually catching something, having to free it and worry about the angry cutting fins and baiting the hook again. But my sister lived for that flash of silver life, longed for it. The fish understood and came to her.

Those years were not always well for us. A sort of madness passed over our family for a while. During the worst of it, my sister and I would escape spiritually into separate reveries in our rooms, sometimes physically as far as the hill of the silver beeches. It was worse for my sister, who had known less of the good times before. I remembered when my parents were young lovers, when they hugged long and hard before my father went to work, and I tried to push in between them, to have a measure of that love. When my sister came, they were already defeated, cautious. I think she was meant to put things back the way they were. She ended up being borne along in the descending flood.

One bad evening, we ran together to the pond in the teeth of an oncoming storm. It was October. Remnant trees shivered their leaves into the air. Most of the forest already stood bare against the black clouds. Piece by piece, the northern sky vanished in the swirl of storm. The grass of the marsh hissed as wind bent it down. My sister ran ahead, and when the road curved me toward the pond, I saw her on its bank dancing with her red hair swirling above her red jacket, dancing with her arms flailing under the gathering tempest, dancing God knew what, fury or hopelessness, or perhaps the possessed jubilation that the spirit knows sometimes outside of any human circumstance. Even with me watching, the Red Dancer kept on until she was exhausted, and the trees bent their heads, and bitter rain bulleted the face of the water.

I still think of the Red Dancer without associating it expressly with my sister. It is a small figure of defiance dancing on a storm-blasted hill. It is who I would have been had I the courage.

A large corrugated pipe pierced the marshward bank of the pond, to carry off floodwater. Rabbits infested it. It would not seem good for rabbits, too big and open to attack at both ends, but something you noticed about that abandoned farm was that it crawled with rabbits. Maybe overpopulation and wet ground forced them into less than ideal habitations. You hung upside down to see how big the shape was inside the tunnel. If it was small, you put your dog at one end and called him to you at the other and had a baby rabbit in your arms in a flash. Adults you let fly past, as they could scratch memorably.

Fed by a forest spring that barely kept even with evaporation, the pond didn't contribute much to Roosevelt Ditch, which could, however, be seen from its banks, gathering, a flat formless maze of marsh water not to be a stream until it hit the Eastwood culvert.

I've lived in the mountains long enough to know that water lies differently in different places. In the mountains, it's channeled. It lies *in*. In stone. In the slashes between mountains. In beds cut deep by rivers old as the world. In the flatlands, it lies *on*. The lips of lakes tremble over their banks, glittering at the underside of air, held in by molecular tension. The faces of ponds shimmer at the level of the grass, overflowing, spillable at the least troubling of the planet, the land too new for it to have worn anywhere to rest.

The glacier's remnant of marsh lay deeper than itself in water, tipping and pouring down invisible inclines toward distant rivers. Like the marshes of the Sudan, its channels wandered, and a safe path yesterday could plunge you knee-deep tomorrow. The scale was small, but so were we, and it was all we needed of wilderness.

Late in winter, thaw and rain turned the marsh into a brimming gray lake, shot the creek through its culvert with a roar audible blocks away. Acre by acre, the lots eastward sank, and the creek bed vanished under an undifferentiated chaos of water, the world unmade, a gray blank to the slope of Tallmadge Hill, a gray blank northward beyond the limits of sight. Bridges and lawn furniture and property and landmarks were lost. The rich woman's white ducks paddled stupidly out into continents of rushing silver. Clumps of willows stood out above the flood, gathering to themselves the flotsam that shot between them hurrying down.

Egyptian papyri tell of the Nile before creation, an infinite nothingness punctuated by complications—perhaps mounds of mud and willow—that could become a world.

I pulled on my boots and waded.

Had I stumbled into the bed of Roosevelt Ditch itself, I'd have been swept away. I'd have ended up with the lumber and barbed wire snagged in the willows. Mother was fond of saying that one could drown in a teacup. Danger was, of course, part of the thrill. Still, I kept some distance from what I thought must be the original bed. I waded with Mr. Bartley's lawn and my father's garden and the glen of the skunk cabbages invisible under my boot soles. I waded with the ever present possibility of being lost forever in my old life, maybe found far down the stream where everything was different. I waded between two firmaments, both dark, one swift and roiled, one curved and weeping over the heads of the willows.

It's difficult to justify my delight. While the storm sewers poured into our basement and chairs and *National Geographic*s and my father's tool-shedding workbench rose toward the ceiling, thumping and bumping in the freezing water, I waded, happy, a lone soul in a world without features and, therefore, the imagination's playground.

Water devoured the backyard. It climbed the trunks of the

crabapples. It added my father's fish pond to itself. If you looked at it right, you'd think that the flood had gushed from that construction as from one of those miraculous inexhaustible pitchers of mythology, bounty and ruin paying us back in equal measure. When the waters fell, my tough old catfish would be gone, finning out to conquer the firmament of water as he had every corner of his tiny artificial universe. I pictured him shouldering among the shrubs and drowned roots of grass, dogs barking as he forced his dim gold between their paws.

I toed the bottom with my boot, not in fear but in expectancy. Earth itself might change beneath my feet. It did not pay to fear, but to be ready. All human things bumped and skidded under the rafts of dislodged ice. The world was going under. What came out again must be new and strange, scoured the way those deluge-releasing deities of Mesopotamia anticipated, a slate swept clean. I deepened the water in my heart until it was those waters in the Bible that run over and under the world. I opened the windows of the silt so to see everything.

Under the clarifying waters, there would be priceless paintings and famous statues, whole museums, film unrolled for the viewing of fish, lost friends, the dead that our parents grieved so over, Amelia Earhart, cannibals, arctic explorers, story heroes, Agamemnon and Jason, the skeletons of cats that wandered out to die in the girlhoods of our grandmothers.

Except for the cold, the primary sensation was aural. I listened to the low song of the waters, sometimes thwarted, sometimes pushing all obstacles away. Music troubled the water, not what sounded like music, maybe, but what black and cold would sing if they had voices. My flood was enveloping the world.

People thinking *flood* think of rushing walls, an irresistible downward violence. But this came slowly, an ill-tacked carpet rising from the floor. The time of flood was a time of finding. Stand looking upstream, and all things drift by. Dip your hand, if you can, into the freezing current. Grip. Bring the treasure to your eyes. Heraclitus had only one truth about the river. I had another. It is ever the same river, reborn as a fountain rebuilds itself in air, *this* water the water that bathed the feet of mastodons, *this* rock the firmness that emerged when chaos cried *enough!* Not a story, this was a truth discovered . . . a truth I could never express to my father, who thrashed downstairs through the flotsam, turning out the gas in the furnace so we wouldn't explode, his face a mask of loss at what the flood had done.

I wake from sleep hundreds of miles away and years after. At morning, there comes a dream of pure waters. Amid the construction at the university campus where I teach, I find, miraculously, a deep pool of crystal water. I manage to save it from the bulldozers, though they cut close enough to give it walls narrow as the cup of a goblet, curved and opaque. A student brings some turtles out of a lab, mud turtles with their shells softened by disease and incarceration and despair. I set the turtles in the deep blue water. They disappear for a moment, then reappear transformed into great sea turtles, silver and pale gold-green, beating the surface with glittering flippers.

I dream of being marooned in a strange city, penniless and frightened. I get a room in a flophouse. The landlord takes me upstairs, unlocks the door to my room but does not open it. I take this as the sign that something horrible lurks within. Nevertheless, I have nowhere to go and so must enter. I step inside. I flip the light switch, which is not an incandescent bulb but the sun, at evening when the light is red, and what it illumines is a great bog, running with clean waters, green with grasses, teeming with fish and turtles, studded with herons, loud with the calling of birds and frogs. I know I am safe. I know all is well. I look for a dry spot to lie down and sleep, and dream the dreams that come within a dream.

I go to the mountain forest to shake dreams from my head, the too many dreams. There, depressions, declivities, the ruts of the tires of off-road vehicles gleam with water the color of the leaves at the bottom. I squat and peer close. The water is lumpy with eggs, globs and thick streamers of eggs, some floating, some massed at the bottom: amphibians, toads, wood frogs, probably salamanders. I stand up, quickly, realizing this is as dank and disturbing as the dreams.

❀

Sixteen years separate me from my last visit to the pond and the hill of the silver beeches. The wait was deliberate, so the fear of seeing would at last become the need to see. To get there now I pass between rows of pastel aluminum houses, down a dead-end road called, nostalgically, Pheasant Run. That there were once pheasants I may be the last one to bear witness. Once beyond the houses, I see as an archaeologist sees, or as a sensitive sees in a trance that reveals past lives. The old road is there, its bordering hills smoothed out but suggested by the living contours of the land. As my father said it would be, the pond is filled in. Yet its round limits are still visible, and the rock-crowned island in its center. If I dug here, I'd find the bones of fish, green ghosts of algae, the fossilizing chitin of dragonfly nymphs.

I continue down the paths I knew. I recite the identities of trees, mostly here great clean beeches, hardly changed, but also the weird cucumber tree the farmer must have planted a century ago, with its red bumpy fruit and its aura of being the last and only one on earth. Their changelessness is a personal blessing as well as an environmental one. In a life without human continuity, I cherish the continuity I can impose on the forest. *You remember me!* I say to the quiet giants, seeing no reason why they couldn't. I make the circuit of the little woods, remembering here the mucky spot to be avoided, here the spring boiling up under its pyramid of rocks, the stand of jewelweed, the carpet of violets, the cucumber tree with its Venusian fruit; there the rusting truck chassis finally gone, the Reading Rock, the Hill of Burials where my mortal pets found their final rest.

Finally I return to the dusty pond bed. I lay my hand flat on the dust, as it once would have lain flat on the fecund water. I will not have it this way. I will the sky to change. I will the ground to return to what it was. I step back, out of the way of deepening water. The dome above me fills with stars, the west grows bloody with the last of some summer day. My sister and I stand staring into the dark pond, flecked indiscriminately with stars and lightning bugs. Terror and delight flow with the cold mist out of the gloom of beeches. We watch, silent, for the mystery we know is coming. Before our eyes the Mother of Turtles heaves her shell over the rim of the pond, plods northward, step by step, seeking the Great Lakes, the one water great enough to contain her.

In its culverts and tunnels, tamed so houses can gobble its flood plain, Roosevelt Ditch continues. My father says it cannot flood anymore, with satisfaction and triumph in his voice, the same tone with which men revealed in ancient times that the thunder and the wildfire were not gods at all.

I lean down and whisper to the sad ring of dust that it is the living water of my boyhood, forever alive now by the power of memory. Does it believe me? It must. It is the only power I have.

The same power that restores the dry pond gives men and women dreams to recover what is lost. I had a dream several years after leaving home. In the dream, I lived again in my father's house by the creek. It was night. I sat with my father watching TV. The door opened and Mother came in, telling us that her death had been a sort of a test that we had passed, and all was well again. Behind her in bright procession came everyone I'd loved and missed. I sat stupefied with the power of forgiveness, undeserved, unasked. Whether I was forgiven or I was doing the forgiving, I didn't know, nor did it matter. Finally, exhausted by joy, I walked out onto the dark lawn. Happy voices filled the house behind me. There was neither moon nor stars. It was a night before heavy summer rain. I heard a sound and looked toward the forest. My little black-and-white dog, Bimbo, the constant companion of my boyhood, ran toward me as he had in life, hind end opposing front end, beaming that uncomplicated love there is no way to repay except to receive. Only then I realized the immensity of the gift. My dog was a flourish, an adornment of a joy that was already perfect, as though the Restorer had said, "You might have forgotten, but I have not."

The best is yet to be told. The gift was not him to me, but me to him. I was his paradise.

To be another creature's paradise was a blessing I had not anticipated. I held my little dog in my arms, listening to the familiar voices in the house, listening at last to one more sound that came out of the night. It was the sound of water. Roosevelt Ditch rose slowly and musically around the foundations of the house, down from the feet of the Mother of Turtles, from the roots of the beeches, from the tangle of the glacier's marsh, up the dark lawn, enfolding my feet and knees, over my head, breathable, restorative, taking my dog and me into itself—a flowing sweetness, a medium of imperishable crystal enfolding and preserving: one moment of perfect joy become the last moment and all moments, enduring, a blessing beyond the heart's power to ask.

17. THE WALL BETWEEN THE WORLDS

At sea's edge
his lyre lies amid the jellyfish.
This is all that remains of famous Orpheus
that man-maddener, that infuriator of women,
who, by all but the maddest accounts,
got what he deserved.

Because of him I think there must be a meter
to justify the longing of brutes, to uplift
even of the puniness of the puny.

Because of him I listen for Tyrannosaur's thunder
in the scolding of the she-wren.

Look little, *he said,* go to hell.

THE DREAMS are like knots on a chain stretching into darkness and mist. You cannot see the end of it. You must follow, knot by knot.

Mother is buying yarn in the Woolworth five-and-ten in Eastgate Plaza. You are bored, and wander to the back of the store, and see—where the drinking fountain used to be—something you have not seen before. There is a door and what lies beyond the door seems to be a silvery, twinkling darkness. You walk through the door and, after a surprisingly brief climb, find yourself on the surface of the moon. The sagging heavens blaze with stars. The blue earth behind you is a dome so immense you wonder what lies hidden beneath the gleaming hemisphere. That you can breathe, that you do not freeze instantly, amazes you less than it probably should.

You mount the stairs of your grandfather's house on Hampton Road, only the stairs do not stop where they used to. They go up, and up, until you are tired and choose one of the doors in the staircase wall. You open it onto the ballroom of a palace. Men and women are dancing in costumes you know from the movies. You could walk out there and join the dance, but beyond the windows of the ballroom is a terrace, and that terrace easing out into a firmament of stars. The stars are not like what you remember, either, but diamond cartwheels, unblinking ranks of eyes, magical jeweled symbols stately, visibly turning in the blue depths. You know you could go out and join the dance, or you could climb higher, get closer to the unimaginable wheels of light. You shut the door on the ball and climb. You can hear the fires singing through the walls, the fires that are the heavenly beings. You realize you have lived your childhood in the Milky Way, and that there is, before such age and immensity, nothing but childhood.

With the visions of splendor comes responsibility. My sister has a dream of me, which she tells in a letter:

I was hiking through the woods behind Eastwood swimming pool one day when I ran into you. I asked why you weren't in Syracuse, at graduate school, like you were supposed to be. You said that you were on a secret mission behind the Gas

Company. You took me there. I found that you were helping mentally unstable children. For some reason, unstable children were being put to death, and the public didn't know about it. You had rescued some of the children and were raising them in the woods. Wizards had made your colony invisible so that you would not be caught, but since I believed in the wizards I could see the colony, and you. I had to stay there once I found you. While I was helping you, you constantly warned me not to bother the wildlife. I didn't listen and went into the woods and jumped on some turtles' backs. You were very upset about it, but I told you that you were foolish. That night, the turtles came into my bed by pulling themselves up the sheets with their mouths and attacked me. I would have died if I hadn't awakened. The dream scared me so much I am still checking my bed sheets before sleep.

There is a flat, wet prairie with clusters of rural buildings in the middle distance. With the logic of a dream, I know the prairie is New Orleans. I meet a young couple with three children. We go to a restaurant the couple remembers from their honeymoon: a long wooden table half-sunk into the yellow grass of the prairie, with low benches on either side. Food appears out of deep trenches in the ground. We put it on the table and eat. The couple tells me of the last time they were at the restaurant, a strange tale, full of mysterious doings and details which seem to go unnoticed by them, but which seem sinister to me. The couple begins to fade, and I realize their bodies have been veils around evil spirits. The light changes, and the table stands now in a deep cavern open to a starry sky. The illumination is by fire licking up through the floor. Though the couple are evil spirits, the three children are real, human, and, when their parents vanish into the darkness, they come to me for comfort. At that moment, I perceive that the older boy and I have already gone through this struggle, that he really is safe far away. I say to the younger boy, "It is not your time yet." He takes on the feathers of a bird and flies through the gap in the ceiling. But the girl I take in my arms. We are assaulted by demons. I know I have to say their complicated names to make them go away. I mispronounce them, and the demons laugh at me each time, declaring that I have failed. They want me to let go of the child in despair. But somehow, miraculously, I know they are lying. Even done badly, the spell has power, and if I hold out against them I know I can save the girl, as I saved her brother in a dream now but half-remembered.

I have to say their complicated names. It doesn't even matter if I say them wrong, but somehow I must wrap my tongue around the hurtful syllables. The word has the power. To utter it correctly is the goal, of course, but even to attempt the utterance contains virtue. I know the saving spell; I must, somehow, gather the strength to say it.

There is an old story:

King Cormac mac Art wanders in the Land of the Immortals. He passes many days and many strange sights one upon the other. On a certain day, he happens upon a noble mansion of white stone and rafters of fragrant cedar. On the roof, a company of men are thatching, not with straw, but with the feathers of a fabulous bird. The men sing as they work. Nearing the end of their task, they see that they have run out of feathers. They all leave the mansion to gather more, and, when they are gone, a great wind blows up from the sea and blasts the roof away. They return, fall down, and lament for a while, then wearily set to thatching as before. Cormac watches this happen several times. He perceives that it has been going on since the Beginning of the world, and will continue to the End.

The king arrives at last at the dwelling of the god Mananan and his wife, the goddess Fand. They take pleasure in showing Cormac the treasures of the house. Fand displays jewels and silverplate, fabrics of cloth-of-the-waters, cloth-of-the-moon. Mananan shows him spears balanced like music, torques and heaps of gold, harps singing in the breezes of the Land of the Immortals. But the most wonderful treasure is a golden cup that shatters into a hundred fragments at the sound of a lie, and flies together again at the uttering of truth.

When they have eaten, Cormac tells the god and goddess of his adventures. He tells them of the mansion where the thatchers try futilely to thatch with feathers. "What, " asks Cormac, "is the meaning of this?"

Mananan answers sadly, "It is an image of the men of this world who seek to find meaning in or rest from their labors, or renown in time to come for what they have accomplished. It is an image of futility."

No sooner had Mananan said these words than the magic cup shattered into a hundred pieces.

"Your explanation, O Mananan," said Cormac, "is not true."

"Nevertheless," the god answered, "it must suffice. The truth of the story must never be told, lest the children of art give over the thatching of the house and let it be covered with common straw."

My chosen vocation certainly looked futile to most of those to whom it was, recklessly, confided. Futile, though not ungallant, not without a certain beauty. That one wished to be a poet was the sort of confession that would get you a pat on the head and a knowing, he'll-grow-out-of-*that* smile. Few people imagine that you can make a living out of simply knowing the right thing to say on those rare occasions when saying the right thing may save the world.

Except for Mrs. Otto, who made us write sonnets and haiku and terza rima, exercises which everyone hated but me, sitting in the front-seat-but-one, with my braces hanging out and my red hair uncombed, begging with my hungry eyes for more.

Except for Mrs. Davidson, whose radar was out for a budding poet, and who lit on me not with the mortifying enthusiasm of some former mentors, not with the suspicion of a rival, but with the pure concern of the teacher. Ellet High was not ready for a poet, and Mrs. Davidson and I kept our secret. I left poems on her desk: epics based on Norse mythology; long psalms to pagan gods and to people I had crushes on and converted into pagan gods; lamentations for people still perfectly alive but more useful to me, poetically, deceased; sonnets; villanelles; haiku. And she returned them marked "wonderful . . . wonderful."

Were they wonderful? Those I have kept are not so bad as one feared, and so full of juice and ambition that one forgives them many of their shortcomings.

By the time I got to Hiram College, the pattern was set. I left my poetry notebook home when I first went, thinking to concentrate on studies and let what was, after all, basically an embarrassing frivolity simmer for a while. I was going to be a chemist. I was going to be a biologist. I was going to be a musician. I was going to be an actor. I was going to be a high school teacher. I fooled people with ever changing answers to the question, "What's your major," wanting to keep my options open, wanting to play behind the veil, because it was none of their damn business.

But I knew the whole time. When I went home at Thanksgiving, the poetry notebook came back with me, never to leave my side again. I was going to be a poet. The studies took care of themselves. I realized I couldn't think right unless I was making poems. It didn't matter what the poems were about. I couldn't concentrate on German unless I was making poems about flowers. I couldn't concentrate on history unless I was writing an epic of Elfland. I couldn't process experience unless I wrote about it. No love without a love poem, no hate without a cleansing diatribe, not even a star cleanly risen in the sky without its welcoming fanfare of words. I was a poetry machine. Nobody knew where my mind spent its labors. The habit of secrecy was as strong as the habit of poetry. After supper, when other students scattered to their evenings, I crept back into Hinsdale Hall. I knew a room at the northwest corner of the building where I would be seen only by the janitor, a room he did last, where I could be alone until long past midnight. While the owls and raccoons hunted in the valley of Silver Creek and the lovers crept to Sugar Camp and the frat boys roared in the club rooms and the Amish buggies clattered home through the streets of Hiram, I sat in my corner and wrote, wrote, wrote. Two poems, four poems, six poems a night, falling asleep with the pen in my hand, waking, adding the next line, drowsing off, startled awake by the door opening suddenly, shutting quietly, and the understanding janitor fussing somewhere else for a minute more so I could eke out one more stanza.

And for the second time in my life, I was utterly happy. I was happy when God came to my bedroom. I was happy when the muse came to the northwest corner of Hinsdale Hall, the second happiness in some ways indistinguishable from the first, in some ways so unlike. I wanted nothing from God but the communion of that hour. From the muse, I wanted all the rest of my life.

Life has run since on the overflow of those two moments of joy, with one further inclusion: sex. This too brought fierce joy, but at a time after what is recounted here, and of a kind so different that it might be considered part of another life. Three times I was happy, then. This is not to complain, but to observe and, perhaps, celebrate. God, poetry, and sex are a trinity not to be sniffed at. I know that millions and millions have never been happy even once. I was so happy having found the practice of my life that I assumed my happiness would last forever, that the path found was all that mattered, that it henceforth would be straight, true, that the Way could not be lost. I was lucky. I was eighteen and knew what I was created to do. I was golden. Strangest of all to tell, I assumed everyone would love me for being so lucky and so golden, that they would love me for being a poet and love me better for being a good one. I don't know what put that into my head, except reflecting on how much I loved poets, imagining that they, my poems in their hands, would be murmuring like Mrs. Davidson *wonderful . . . wonderful . . .* and admit me to their circle.

I forget sometimes that I'm not the last poet the world will ever make, not even the last poet Akron made. Sometimes I think all the gods of poetry hold their breath, waiting for me to make the next move. Then I see their attention waver, their glances dart over my shoulder at someone coming up behind:

The sun sinks under North Hill. The patients on the western side of St. Thomas Hospital cover their faces against the rush of light, but they do not close the blinds. Who knows how many more flamingo sunsets there will be? Who knows how many red clouds settling on the western plain like the Last Judgment?

The red-gold light steamrolls Fairlawn, explodes against the towers of downtown, vacant now, gazing with blank eyes out onto the empty streets. It roars up Market and Exchange, consumes the cars hurrying home on the expressway. The window of City Hospital inside which I was born goes up in gold light. The leaves of Maytree go gold above, emerald below, all deepening into blue, into purple as the light sinks. Swallows skim the surface of Alder Pond. The ancient heron curls cronelike beside the water, pecking at a last glimmer of fins.

A kid comes through the front door after a day's work. He's grimy, tired. He reaches for the TV remote, but the light against his window is a voice, and he lets the remote drop. He goes to his room. The voices are about him, the grandfathers, the grandmothers, the heroes, the demigods that brought his clan down from heaven to struggle and exile, forward uncertainly to this hour of peace.

He closes the door. Sits down.

He arches his hands above the keyboard.

He waits.

ABOUT THE AUTHOR

Born and raised in Akron, Ohio, David Brendan Hopes now lives in Asheville, North Carolina, where he is Professor of Literature at the University of North Carolina and director of Urthona Press, the Black Swan Theater Company, and the Downtown School of the Arts. After completing his BA at Hiram College, Hopes earned an MA at Johns Hopkins University and an MA and PhD at Syracuse University. His first book of poems, *The Glacier's Daughters,* won the Juniper Prize and the Saxifrage Prize. He has published a nonfiction book, *A Sense of the Morning,* and a second collection of poetry, *Blood Rose.*

ABOUT THE BOOK

A Childhood in the Milky Way was designed and typeset on a MacIntosh in QuarkXPress by Kachergis Book Design of Pittsboro, North Carolina. The typeface, Columbus MT, was designed by Patricia Saunders in 1992.

A Childhood in the Milky Way was printed on sixty-pound Writers Natural and bound by McNaughton and Gunn Lithographers, Inc., of Saline, Michigan.